First published in Great Britain in 2021 by Wren & Rook

ISBN: 978 1 5263 6341 1

10 9 8 7 6 5 4 3 2 1

Wren & Rook
An imprint of
Hachette Children's Group
Part of Hodder & Stoughton
Carmelite House
50 Victoria Embankment
London EC4Y 0DZ

A Hachette UK Company
www.hachette.co.uk
www.hachettechildrens.co.uk

Publishing Director: Debbie Foy
Art Director: Laura Hambleton
Designer: Claire Yeo

Printed in China

Clare Balding

FALL OFF GET BACK ON KEEP GOING

ILLUSTRATED BY *Jessica Holm*

wren
&rook

Contents

For Tierney & Karris,
who never cease to inspire me.
J.H

For Flora,
who always gets back on.
C·B

HOW TO FALL OFF ... AND GET BACK ON

Have you ever fallen off your bike, tripped over the dog, stumbled while carrying something (as I did last week with a tray of tea and biscuits), burned the toast you were supposed to be keeping your eye on, spilled jam on your best jumper, fluffed a crucial pass in a football match, forgot your lines in the school play or mucked up in a maths test?

It happens.

The trick is to know how to recover.

Stumble and correct yourself. Trip and recover your balance. Make a mistake and learn from it. Drop something and catch it before it smashes (or mend it when it does).

In short, *learn how to fall off and get back on.*

I want to help you recover from your mistakes and grow stronger from the experience. Because, believe me, I've been there.

I want you to know how to keep going and be at the top of your game in every situation. Why?

So that you can:
- be a great teammate
- be an excellent friend
- enjoy school more
- be the best you can be
- get the most out of life, whatever happens along the way!

In this book we'll look at 10 different parts of your character that can help you embrace mistakes and move on from them. They are things like patience, confidence, courage, kindness and resilience (my favourite word for this is 'stickability' – more on this later).

Think of all these parts of your character as ingredients for a great big delicious cake. Some of the things you've probably already got in the cupboard, others you'll discover as we go through this book. And together, we can make a cake that is light and tasty (and doesn't have a soggy bottom!). Everyone's cake will be different and that's just as it should be.

delicious
cake

But, first of all, let me tell you a bit about me. My name is Clare. I present stuff on the TV and on the radio. You might have seen me at the dog show, Crufts, surrounded by mischievous four-legged friends (I love dogs, as you'll find out …), or at the Olympics, the Paralympics or Wimbledon. I'm the one who interviews people and tells you what's been going on.

OK. That's what I DO … but who AM I?

The number one thing to know about me is that I'm a really happy, positive person. I'm like a dog who can't stop wagging its tail. I love my job, I love my wife, I love my life. I like people, I enjoy watching and playing sport and (as I said before) I ADORE animals. I am adventurous, I love a challenge and I certainly always try to be kind and supportive of others.

But the other thing to know about me is that when I was younger, I really struggled. I was impatient, insecure, selfish, frightened of being different and, like an unhappy dog, I probably snapped at a few people along the way.

⊰ LIFE IN LOCKDOWN ⊱

The spring and summer of 2020 was probably very different to anything you've ever experienced before.

You may have missed seeing your friends, playing in the park, going on trips, and seeing your grandparents and other family. You might even have missed being at school – and you probably thought that would NEVER happen.

So, what did you do to keep yourself going?

- Go for walks
- Jump on your bike and head off to explore the neighbourhood
- Speak to your grandparents and friends through video calls
- Do family quizzes
- Learn to bake
- Join in with the Joe Wicks exercise classes every morning?

If you were leaving primary school it probably felt as if you were wrenched away before you were ready. It was a confusing, scary, uncertain time when no one knew whether life would ever return to 'normal'. You had to learn to how to do schoolwork in a different way and work out a rhythm and a routine to the day that wasn't defined by bells going off at the end of a lesson or a timetable that mapped out everything for you.

We all had to learn to try and concentrate when there were loads of distractions. It was a struggle sometimes to stay focused on one thing, and that could be really frustrating.

I had to learn to live a different way because all of the sporting events I was supposed to be presenting – the annual Boat Race on the River Thames, the tennis at Wimbledon, the Olympics and Paralympics in Tokyo – were postponed or cancelled.

I had to reset my outlook on things, be thankful for my health and learn to enjoy time passing a little more slowly. It was nice to wear the same comfortable clothes every day, to enjoy the simple things in life, like a walk in the sunshine or listening to the birds singing and not to be rushing around from one event to another. As my presenting jobs were cancelled, I wasn't 'on show' so I didn't even need to wear make-up. Or high heels (that was a relief!). And, of course, it meant I got some precious time to think about the things that make us happier in life.

⇒ IT'S OK TO GET IT WRONG ⇐

I have been a TV and radio presenter for all of my adult life and, believe
me, it doesn't always go to plan. I have messed up live on air in front
of millions of people, I have been criticised by complete strangers on
social media and in the newspapers. I have done things that I *really,
really* wished I could take back – but you can't press 'delete' in real life.
One thing I've learned from all of this is that getting it wrong is part of
the deal – I have had to learn from it and move on.

In my job, I've been incredibly lucky to have seen some of the most
impressive, inspirational and awe-inspiring sporting performances.
I've also seen some heart-breaking losses and awful injuries.

I've seen a lot of people 'fall off'.

I've also watched them get back on and have another go. Many times,
they are even better after their major loss or their big fall. I know that
I have learned a lot from these great sportspeople, and others in the
non-sporting world, too.

When you fall off – and you will – the 10 qualities that make up the
following chapters will be brilliant to have in your toolkit, and I hope
they will help you to get back on and keep going.

By the end of this book, I hope you will feel stronger, braver, kinder and happier.

Do we have a deal?

Let's get going then.

SUPER-STICKY STICKABILITY

1

'I really think a champion is defined not by their wins, but by how they can recover when they fall'.

SERENA WILLIAMS, TENNIS CHAMPION

I was lucky enough to grow up in the countryside, surrounded by beautiful horses and gorgeous dogs. My dad had a weird job – he trained racehorses.

He did what, I hear you say? OK, let me explain ...

A racehorse trainer is a bit like being a football manager or a netball coach, except with horses. He didn't train them for the circus or to act in films, he trained them to gallop super-fast around a racecourse, ideally faster than the other horses so that they would win.

But the thing to know about my dad is that it was him who taught me an awful lot about

falling off and getting back on again.

≳ FEARLESS FALLING ≲

I was a toddler when I had my first serious fall. No surprise there, you might think. All toddlers fall over a lot, don't they? Well, yes, but wait, there's more …

On this particular day, Dad was meant to be in charge of me. Although he is *exceptionally* good at looking after horses, he's not very good at looking after people.

I think of my dad as a bit like a grown-up child. It wouldn't occur to him to do the shopping, the cleaning or mow the lawn. He wouldn't know how to buy furniture, clothes, do the laundry or pay bills. As for cooking, well, that's not a good idea either. He once tried to warm up milk by putting it in the kettle and boiling it. The kettle was ruined, the milk went everywhere and Mum was furious.

So the one and only time Dad was left in charge of me when I was young, I ended up in hospital.

Let me explain how this happened …

I started riding before I could even walk. My mum said it was quicker and easier to take me places on a tiny pony than to push me in a pram. So one morning, at the age of two and a half, I'd been popped on top of a pony to go and watch the horses

18

on the gallops (which is where the racehorses are trained). My mum had to go somewhere, so she asked Dad to get me safely home. Dad, being Dad, didn't really know how to do this, so he patted my pony on the bottom and off she trotted in the vague direction of home, with me bouncing about on top.

If you've got little brothers and sisters, you might have noticed that they don't have a lot of balance at the age of two and a bit, so I lasted about 60 seconds before I slid off the pony and hit the ground with a thump. I was quite a brave young child, but on this occasion I screamed in shock and pain. I was red in the face and sobbing uncontrollably, so Dad picked me up, put me back in the saddle and said:

'Life is all about falling off and getting back on again, Clarey Bow (which is what he called me) Come on, you're fine.'

But something was hurting. It turns out that I'd broken the small bone that connects the shoulder and the breastbone. It's called the collarbone, and if you feel just below your neck to the side, you'll find it. I had to go to hospital, but I was home again that day.

Dad told me it was a triumph to have broken the bone that professional jockeys (those people in brightly coloured tops who get paid to ride racehorses) are always breaking. It's a well-known 'fact' in the racing world that you can't be *a proper jockey* until you've broken your collarbone.

And I'd done it before I was even three years old …

And as I got a bit older, something that Dad was keen to remind me was that the other qualification for being a 'proper jockey' was to fall off a hundred times.

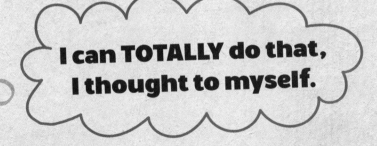

I can TOTALLY do that, I thought to myself.

So every morning before school, when I climbed aboard our Shetland pony, Valkyrie, I would fall straight back off again. I fell off sideways, backwards, forwards, and even jumped on and straight off the other side with barely a second in the saddle. It must have driven my mum mad. But in the following days, I got extremely good at falling and rolling. Instead of tensing up and freezing to prevent a tumble, I relaxed and let it happen.

Before long, I had reached the proud target of ONE HUNDRED falls.

'**I did it.**' I beamed Dad a winning smile and waited for the praise to come my way. '**Did what?**'

'I fell off a hundred times. AND I've already broken my collarbone so that means I'm now A PROPER JOCKEY.' I puffed out my chest with pride and looked around the room. The dogs nodded their approval and I had never felt so chuffed with myself.

The serious point about this story is that I might have got a few bruises along the way, but I realised it was OK to fall off. It's part of learning any skill. If you're going to try as hard as you can at anything, you're going to make mistakes along the way. And this applies not only to falling off a pony or a bike, but to anything you try in your life.

FALL is only one letter different from FAIL – and I've always reckoned that the difference between falling and failing is in your stickability, or your resilience, staying power, perseverance, ability to recover quickly from difficulties, your toughness … call it what you will.

In other words, your real success is in falling off, getting back on and keeping going!

$\gtrsim$ THE SKY'S THE LIMIT $\lessgtr$

Sky Brown is a skateboarding sensation. She has been riding a board since the age of 4 and is the youngest professional in her sport in the whole world.

Skateboarding was due to enter the Olympics for the first time in Tokyo, in the summer of 2020, and Sky was all set to head there as part of the British team, not long after her 12th birthday. Then the Games were delayed a year due to the coronavirus outbreak.

That seemed bad luck for Sky, but sometimes what looks like the worst thing can actually be a blessing. Sky had an epic crash during training in June 2020, which was so awful it would have ruled her out of the Olympics if they had taken place on the original date.

She was practising a hairy move that meant she had to leap from one half-pipe ramp over a gap and onto another. Sky became disconnected with her board and fell, head-first, on to a concrete floor. She put her arm out to break the fall, but she still fractured her skull, broke her left wrist and hand, suffered concussion and severe bruising. Her father said she was lucky to be alive.

Usually when Sky has a wipeout, she tries to forget about it, but this time, she shared a video of her 'worst fall yet' on her official social media channels and recorded a message from her hospital bed, complete with a shiner of a black eye. She said:

'It's **OK** to fall sometimes and I'm just going to get back up and **push** even harder.'

Sky Brown, the young skateboarding prodigy, is proof that even the best are going to fall. But what sets her apart is her determination to get back on her board again and keeping going … all the way to the Olympics. The rearranged date means she has a chance to fully recover and reset herself, and as it happens, she will still be the youngest ever British competitor at a summer Olympic Games. Timing is everything.

≥ HICCUPS, BUMPS AND FALLS ≤

Not everything in life goes smoothly. Everyone (and this includes me, as you will find out through this book!) hits bumps in the road, has hiccups along the way, falls off or falls over.

But stickability isn't about *not* falling off. It's about knowing that if you're trying your very hardest, the chances are that at some point, you WILL fall off. Stickability is about being tough enough to get back up, get back on, and keep trying.

GET BACK UP
GET BACK ON
KEEP TRYING

When I was at school, we had to read out loud in class and as soon as we made a mistake, the teacher would shout, 'CHANGE!' and it would be the turn of the next person. It was quite tough and really nerve-wracking because if you made even the slightest hesitation or stumble

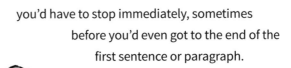

you'd have to stop immediately, sometimes before you'd even got to the end of the first sentence or paragraph.

I was a bit rubbish at it to start with. I'd get nervous and try so hard not to make a mistake that I would immediately forget how to pronounce the simplest word!

'CHANGE!' The teacher would shout, and I wouldn't get another chance for ages. So I decided to practise. I started reading books out loud all the time so that I got used to the sound of my own voice, and if I could see a word coming up that I was unsure about, I'd slow down instead of speeding up. I told myself that I could do this, rather than scolding myself about making mistakes. I tried again and again until, finally, I could read for pages in front of the class without hearing the dreaded word 'Change!'.

Even people who have made it to the TOP of their game have to learn this lesson.

Steve Jobs was one of the most successful American businessmen of all time, co-founding the tech giant Apple (you've heard of the iPod, iPhone and iPad, the Mac computer, right …?)

In his early years, Steve was a perfectionist who needed everything to look and be *exactly* as he wanted it. He always wanted to get his own way. This eventually led to disagreements within Apple, and Steve left.

But he 'got back on and kept going' by focusing his energies on a new company called Pixar. Films like *Toy Story*, *Finding Nemo* and *The Incredibles* were just some of Pixar's global successes! Some years later, Steve Jobs ended up back as CEO (the boss) of Apple, by which time he had discovered, through his own experience of 'falling off', that he couldn't be such a perfectionist with other people's work. He needed to accept that he and his team would make mistakes as a natural part of trying their best.

Steve Jobs had learned that it's OK to fail sometimes, you just need to get back up and keep going.

Stickability is important in every area of our lives.

Have you heard of the famous Mexican artist and feminist icon **FRIDA KAHLO**? Frida was badly injured in a bus crash at the age of 18. She was in hospital for months, encased in a full-body cast, unable to move. She was stuck. But her parents made her a special easel, which meant she could paint while she was lying down. She found the strength to paint self-portraits as a way of understanding herself better, as well as portraying her culture and heritage. When she left the hospital, she was still hampered by intense pain and suffered from it throughout her life, but she used her resilience (or stickability) to inspire her colourful, vivid and breathtaking art.

OUR STICKABILITY TOOLKIT

① Find Your Support Squad

This could be family members (even your annoying brother or sister), friends, trusted teachers or coaches, or school counsellors. Find squad members who are willing to listen and support you. Tell them when you are worried or overwhelmed, or just need some help to find a way through a tricky problem or situation. Let them know that you will become part of *their* support squad, too. We all need one!

② Talk Nicely to Yourself

Sometimes we can be our own worst enemy in the way that we speak to ourselves. We wouldn't dream of saying to our best friends some of the things that we sometimes find ourselves saying in our own heads! If you realise you're saying negative things about yourself (either out loud or in your head) just stop, take a breath and re-set. When you say kind and positive things to yourself, you change the course of your thoughts in that direction.

③ Make a Gratitude Jar

Get an old glass jar and place beside it some strips of paper and pens. Every day, write down one small thing that you are grateful for that day. It could be walking by the river, eating a delicious doughnut or snuggling on the sofa to watch a movie with your family. Not only does this act as a record of little things that you've enjoyed, but when you are feeling a bit short on resilience, you can go back to your jar and remind yourself of some lovely things to do that will boost your stickability!

PATIENCE
IS YOUR
SUPERPOWER

2

'Patience is a key element of success.'
BILL GATES,
ENTREPRENEUR AND TECH PIONEER

When I was younger I was always in a hurry. I just couldn't see the point in waiting for things. I wanted to get on with it, and if I had to wait I thought I was just wasting time. I was impatient on long journeys and was always the one who asked the inevitable:

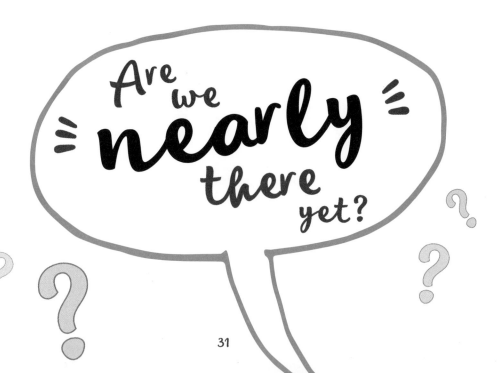

Are we **nearly** there yet?

I simply needed to know how long a journey would take. 'How many minutes is that?' I'd ask. I'd wait a while and then say, 'How many minutes now?' Looking back, I must have driven my mum mad.

Technology has helped speed everything up so that now if we want to watch something, buy something, send a message, talk to someone, or find out the answer to a question, we can press a button or click a mouse and it's (almost) instantly there. In fact, it's so quick and easy that we don't have to be patient about a lot of things.

So why is patience so important?

Well, in my experience, patience is not just about waiting for things, it's about doing things with focus and care. It's about working at something and not being afraid to do it again and again, until you get it right. It's about not expecting everything to come to you at once, but waiting for other people, or for the right time. It's about showing self-control when you feel frustrated or impatient.

⋛ FLOSSY AND THE HIGH-FIVE ⋚

I'm a bit embarrassed now to admit it, but growing up I often only showed patience when it came to animals. Animals are my 'thing' and in truth I often found it easier to be patient with dogs, cats, horses – even snails – than I did with humans.

Flossy, my boxer dog, had a wrinkly face and deep-brown eyes. When she was happy, she smiled and wiggled her whole bottom. I would often lie in her dog bed with her, just as a way of hanging out with her. She made me feel calm and protected.

Flossy was my friend and I wanted to play with her all the time. She was a really sweet dog, but she wasn't keen on learning new tricks.

Not put off by this, I tried to teach her all sorts of things:
- Fetching a ball (she ran around with it in her mouth but never brought it back to me)
- Jumping over a pole I'd balanced between two chairs (she went under it)
- Crawling through a homemade tunnel (she went round it)
- Weaving through bending poles (she ran in the opposite direction)

I once tried to teach her to put her paw in the air like a doggy high-five. But boxers are not the most obedient dogs and if they can't see the point of what you're trying to teach them, they won't do it. So I set about tempting Flossy with a treat. I held it in my hand and put on my firmest voice. Then I put my hand out as if inviting her to high-five. 'Paw,' I said.

Flossy looked at me as if I was an alien who had just landed from outer space. She licked my hand and looked pleased with herself. She clearly didn't understand. I could have given up there and then. I could have taken her outside to play and forgotten all about it, but I didn't want to give up. I knew that Flossy was never going to win an obedience class at Crufts but I wanted to get this one thing right.

So we tried again and again.

An hour later, she finally high-fived me! I hugged her in appreciation. We had both shown patience, kept trying and eventually, Flossy the boxer had done it. I knew she might not do it again tomorrow, but right now, in this moment, we had succeeded in achieving something together. And it felt good.

I ran round the garden in celebration and Flossy jumped up at me, sharing the excitement without necessarily knowing what it was all about. She wagged her whole bottom and smiled at me. What a moment.

I couldn't have been **prouder** if I'd **climbed** Mount Everest, landed on the moon or **jumped** off the top diving board.

It wasn't about the size of the achievement – it was about the effort I'd put into it and the thrill of making it work.

High Five!

⤜THE YEAR OF SPORTING PATIENCE⤛

For athletes, 2020 was a year when they had to dig deep and be very patient. The Olympics and the Paralympics were postponed, so all their training, which had been carefully planned to peak at the Tokyo Games in the summer of 2020, had to be completely re-thought or re-scheduled.

For most of them, it was the first time they'd ever had time off competition without an injury. They didn't have to worry about whether or not they would get back in a team, whether they would lose their ranking, whether they would have to watch someone else triumph while they sat at home. *Everyone* was sitting at home. *Everyone* pressed pause. *Everyone* had to be patient.

Swimmers had to be really inventive because they weren't allowed to go to the local pool. So do you know what some of them did? They bought giant paddling pools and tied special bungee ropes (called swim belts) around their bodies so that they could swim hard on the spot.

Alistair Brownlee has swum every day of his life since he was eight years old, usually at the local pool near where he lives in Yorkshire. Luckily, the double-Olympic-triathlon-gold-medallist had planned for what might happen if he couldn't get to a pool or swim in a lake. He had installed a deep, 5-metre-long bathtub in his garage, with a machine that created strong waves that he could swim against.

Lots of incredibly patient amateur triathletes, who would ordinarily have spent the summer swimming, cycling and running at competitions around the world, did their own versions at home.

Charlotte Raubenheimer from South Africa was meant to be raising money for a charity by competing in an Ironman triathlon (an extended, really tough version of the swim/cycle/run combination). As with many other sporting events, it got cancelled, so she did her very own Ironman at home. That meant swimming in a tiny pool for 2.4 miles. It meant cycling on a stationary bike for 112 miles and then running a full marathon (26.2 miles) in her back garden. She got dizzy from turning so many corners (she made more than 1,500 turns) but 13 hours and 13 minutes after she started, Charlotte completed her 'at home' Ironman for charity.

Climbers who were hoping to compete in the first-ever Olympic rock-climbing competition started climbing inside (and outside!) their own houses. You might have heard some people say they were 'climbing the walls' during lockdown, but these guys actually meant it!

For many athletes it was a major test of their patience and determination. The cancelled sporting events meant that they had to find ever-more-inventive ways to get back on and just

KEEP GOING.

GAME CHANGERS ▶

Roger Federer is the most elegant and graceful tennis player I have ever seen. He moves like a ballet dancer and seems to have more time to play his shots than any of his rivals. But the winner of 20 Grand Slam titles and 8 Wimbledon championships was not always so cool, calm and collected. In his younger days, he had a temper and often got thrown out of practice sessions. In matches he would sometimes shout and break his racket in fury at his own mistakes.

His turning point was when he saw a replay of one of his best winning matches as a Junior. He and his opponent were both behaving badly: shouting, smashing rackets and generally looking miserable. He was embarrassed. He realised that throwing rackets around didn't help him win matches; he needed to conserve his strength for the game itself, to think clearly under pressure and concentrate all his energy on beating his opponent.

It dawned on Federer that there is power in being patient and he decided to control his temper, rather than let frustration, anger and impatience be in control of him.

'I think once you find that peace, that place of peace and quiet, or harmony ... or confidence – that's when you start playing your best.'

ROGER FEDERER

⇒ BACK TO NATURE ⇐

Watch any animal creeping stealthily while hunting prey, or working industriously to build its home or gather food for its young. Watch any tree or flower slowly but surely burst into life and you will truly be able to admire the natural world's sense of timing. Nature doesn't rush.

Evolution takes time.

Sir David Attenborough is the king of natural history. When he talks, we should always listen. He is legendary for his patience while observing and reporting on species from every corner of the animal kingdom. All the award-winning documentary series he presents take an incredible amount of time to produce. Often a project will be three or four years in the making, with camera operators in multiple locations sometimes waiting for days to capture the two-minute shot that will make us TV viewers gasp in wonder.

Nature and the natural world is David Attenborough's 'thing'. His passion is so strong that patience comes naturally to him. Likewise, animals are my 'thing' and because I love being with them so much,

I don't ever feel that my time is being wasted if it is spent teaching an animal something or helping it adapt to a different situation. As I found out with Flossy the boxer, I can be very patient when doing something I love, so the trick I use is to try to transfer my patience superpower into all the different areas of my life. Try it – it works!

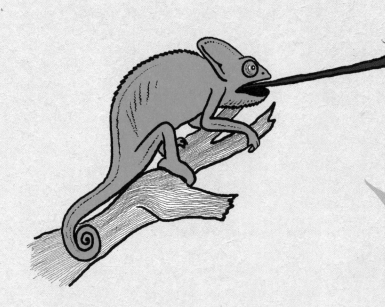

'Sometimes, it's hours and hours of absolutely nothing happening and you just have to sit there and wait and hope that your instincts and your natural history knowledge will pay off in the end.'

SIR DAVID ATTENBOROUGH

⇊ WHAT'S YOUR 'THING'? ⇊

Think about something you love doing: cycling, dancing, playing an instrument, football, shooting basketball hoops, cooking, maths, gaming, drawing, painting, skateboarding.

If you find you can be patient when doing something you love, transfer your **'patience superpower'** to things that make you feel frustrated or impatient.

In other words, use the patience you reserve for the stuff you like doing for the stuff you don't …

> *It's all about doing what I love. I'm relaxed and enjoying what I'm doing and when the goals come you have more fun.*
>
> **SAM KERR, CAPTAIN OF THE AUSTRALIAN NATIONAL WOMEN'S SOCCER TEAM**

(Practically) PERFECT PATIENCE

These are some tips for things that I do when I'm feeling impatient or when I simply need to calm myself, exercise self-control, settle my nerves or just be 'in the moment'. Try a few of them when you need to – they really do work!

1 Take a deep breath in through your nose and count to 5 as you breathe out. Let the air out slowly through pursed lips, as though you are blowing through a straw.

2 Move your head round in a circle, one way and then the other. Roll your shoulders 5 times, shake your hands out.

3 Move your hips from side to side. Then rotate your feet (one at a time if you're standing up!).

4 Look out of the window or around you and notice every detail: colours, textures, smells, sounds; the way things move or how the clouds are chasing across the sky.

5 Count to 10 and back down to zero. Remember to take lots of slow, deep breaths.

Patience helps us to anticipate and enjoy things more. It helps us concentrate better. It helps us save our energy and be more productive.

Patience can be our

SECRET SUPERPOWER!

3

'Just believe in yourself.
Even if you don't, pretend that you
do and, at some point, you will.'

VENUS WILLIAMS

It's a big day. You've been building up to it all week, nervous about the moment when you are expected to be at your best in front of other people. Imagine yourself waking up and getting dressed. What do you put on? Pants (clean, obviously); socks (matching, ideally). Your other clothes (it's a good idea not to go out just in pants and socks). You clean your teeth and smile into the mirror.

Oh, and then finally you put on your **Cloak of Confidence.**

What? You mean you didn't see that cloak hanging in your wardrobe? Well, here's the big secret I'm going to share with you. Your Cloak of Confidence has been there all along, just waiting to be worn at the times when you most need it.

Because confidence can be worn, just like a superhero's cloak.

You can wear it for all sorts of occasions, from big to small.

Big ones might be:

- walking into a room full of strangers
- striding onto the stage for your school play
- lining up in a race on sports day
- taking an exam

And small ones might be:

- saying hi to someone new
- joining in a conversation
- sitting down to write a story
- wearing new glasses for the first time

Maybe these aren't such big life events, but whenever things mean a lot, we can get nervous. Some of us are naturally shy, others don't mind so much. Feeling nervous about things is good because it helps you understand what you care about. So if you're feeling nervous, wearing the Cloak of Confidence will help. That's a manufacturer's guarantee …

HAND CRAFTED JUST FOR YOU, ALL NATURAL, MADE FROM 100% CONFIDENCE, WASH AT 30 DEGREES! DO NOT TUMBLE DRY!

Your Cloak of Confidence shows you that confidence is often an invisible skill that anyone can learn. It's all about believing in yourself.

⋛ON BOARD A BIG, HAIRY BEAST!⋜

I sometimes struggled at school. I felt I was rubbish at maths, I hated not being picked for the netball team, and I was teased for smelling of horse manure (I don't think I did, by the way) or for wearing the wrong clothes (what was wrong with my flares, anyway?). I had braces on my teeth and food always got stuck in them, so I tried not to smile so that no one would see. I missed my dog all the time at school – she always wagged her tail and was pleased to see me, whatever I was wearing. She didn't notice my braces.

I felt that I just didn't fit in. Maybe it should have made me miserable and I think it would have done, except for one thing.

You see, I loved horses, and they loved me.

The only time that I felt truly confident was when I was around horses. I understood them and that helped me feel confident about myself. Confidence is very important when you're around animals – it helps them believe that you know what you're doing and it means they will trust you.

My favourite pony was called Frank. Together, he and I could gallop, jump over fences and weave our way through any tricky situation. I learned how to sit securely in the saddle, look ahead for potential problems, react quickly and, above all, keep calm. I could do things on horseback that I could never do in any other situation. I felt empowered and uplifted. It helped that I was five feet up in the air on board a big hairy beast, but it was my 'safe place'. I count myself incredibly lucky that I had the chance to grow up around horses and that I could build my confidence this way.

And when things would go wrong, I'd tell myself:
'I can ride. At least I can ride.'

And this became my mantra. A mantra is something you say to yourself over and over again to give yourself a sense of calm. My mantra helped me find my confidence, even when I wasn't sat in a saddle, and it became important to me as I grew older; it helped me recover from all sorts of falls …

You may not be able to (or want to) ride a horse, but believe me when I say that you can find your own confidence.

'SAFE PLACE'.

'I CAN RIDE. AT LEAST I CAN RIDE.' 'I CAN RIDE.' 'I CAN RIDE. AT LEAST I CAN RIDE.' 'I CAN RIDE.' 'I CAN RIDE. AT LEAST I CAN RIDE.' 'I CAN RIDE.' 'I CAN RIDE. AT LEAST I CAN RIDE.' 'I CAN RIDE.' 'I CAN RIDE. AT LEAST I CAN RIDE.' 'I CAN RIDE.' 'I CAN RIDE. AT LEAST I CAN RIDE.' 'I CAN RIDE.' 'I CAN RIDE. AT LEAST I CAN RIDE.' 'I CAN RIDE.' 'I CAN RIDE. AT LEAST I CAN RIDE.' 'I CAN RIDE.' 'I CAN RIDE. AT LEAST I CAN RIDE.'

49

CHANGING SCHOOLS

I went to the local primary school in my village, but at age 10 I started at a girls' boarding school. I felt totally out of place. I was younger than everyone else and smaller, too. Most of the girls seemed much more advanced than me in many of the subjects we studied. They were also better than me at sport.

For the first time in my life, my mantra couldn't help me. 'I can ride' didn't count any more because I could no longer see or ride my pony. I was on my own and out of my depth. I tried to keep up by copying others. I started by copying Emma, who was the scruffiest girl in the school. She pulled her jumper sleeves down below her hands and wore her shirt untucked. She was always being told to smarten up, but she didn't care. Then I copied Bex, who seemed much more grown-up than everyone else. She was tall and really elegant. I tried to walk like her, following her down the corridor (without her noticing, obviously – that would have been weird!) so that I could move with her swagger and swing my arms like she did.

Finally – and this is what really got me into trouble – I really, really wanted to be part of the cool gang of girls. They dared each other to do more and more outrageous things, breaking the rules whenever they could and getting away with it. Then, they dared me to steal things from the local shop …

Maybe it was inevitable that I would be the one who got caught.

I was called in to see the headmistress. She told me that the village shop had a video camera. They had seen me stealing things. To my horror, I was suspended from school, and when I came back the following term, I felt ashamed and embarrassed. I didn't want to get out of bed in the mornings. It seemed like every pupil was staring at me and I was sure I could hear people whispering.

'There she goes. The thief.'

The jokes all seemed to be at my expense.

'Here, Clare, have a spoon – it's made of "steal"! Geddit?'

I was labelled as the shoplifter. I couldn't escape the feeling of shame. That would be my identity for the rest of my school days.

Unless I could change things.

I kept quiet for most of that first term back at school. I tried not to get into trouble, I concentrated on my work, I played sport and didn't cry when I got hit by a stray lacrosse* stick or ball. I made myself invisible. I read books endlessly and started to get better marks in English, the only subject I felt I was any good at. I had a very good teacher, which helped. She gave me encouragement and made me feel that I wasn't stupid.

*in case you don't know what lacrosse is, try to imagine it as Quidditch but without the broomsticks!

I started to develop a tiny bit of self-belief. It happened so slowly that I barely even noticed, like a tomato seed gradually growing into a little green ball, and then getting bigger and bigger until it ripens and turns red. Through finding what I was good at, I was learning an important lesson. Confidence isn't all about being the loudest or showing off. The quietest people in the world can be the most confident. I adapted my lucky mantra. Instead of 'I can ride' it became 'I can read'.

I could escape into different worlds by reading books and I found that in English lessons, I could voice my opinion and everyone listened. Eventually, the other girls started to include me in games or invite me to sit with them at lunch or to watch TV.

The one shadow hanging over me was that I still felt as if I could never totally reinvent myself. Everyone at school knew my terrible secret. My identity as a shoplifter was sealed for life and it would never change. **Or would it?**

⋛ A TURNING POINT ⋚

A couple of years later, our school went on an outdoor adventure trip to the Lake District. It was meant to be a week of challenges designed to take us out of our comfort zone, to build a sense of team spirit and to help us make new friends.

We had an instructor who had never met me before and didn't know a thing about my history. He didn't care what I had or hadn't done in the past. All that mattered was how I behaved on his course – whether I was a good team member, whether I was brave and committed, whether I could motivate others to get to the end of a tough challenge like building a raft, getting through a rope assault course or abseiling down a cliff face.

That instructor, Mr Evans, changed my life. He believed in me and I wanted to do well for him, so I threw myself into every challenge, helping others along the way and making sure our team always finished together.

He taught me the joy of focusing on other people, encouraging them and motivating them to finish a task that might be really frightening for them. I didn't really think about myself, I thought about my team.

Mr Evans' report from that adventure trip gave me a fresh start. It was so good that it persuaded my school to make me Head of House. Less than a year later, the teachers and all the pupils voted for their new Head Girl …

I had gone from being the most *despised girl* in the school to being HEAD GIRL.

I used to wish that I could have changed things so that I had never shoplifted and, believe me, I don't want you to try it, but there will be other things that go wrong in your life that you feel will hang over you for ever. My message is that it doesn't have to be that way. I wonder now if maybe my life wouldn't have worked out the way it has if I hadn't known humiliation and rejection. Maybe I needed that to work out my true identity, rather than following the crowd.

I think I needed that experience of falling and getting back up to show me how to keep going and achieve my best.

We have all done things we regret or have said hurtful things. We all feel alone and rejected at times.

EVERY. SINGLE. ONE OF US.

It's what you do with that regret that counts. Do you fight those emotions or try to understand them and realise they will pass?

(Hint – you never win a fight with emotions – their boxing gloves are better than yours!)

There is *always* a way back to confidence, and you'll find your own way of 'getting back on', perhaps when you're least expecting it.

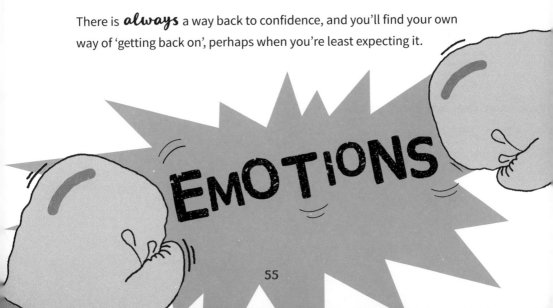

LIGHTNING BOLT

What's the first thing you think of when you hear the name of the world record-breaking sprinter, **Usain Bolt**? I bet you think of his 'Lightning Bolt' pose, his body sideways, one arm drawn back and one pointing forward as if firing an arrow. Did you know, by the way, that it comes from a Jamaican dancehall move?

When Bolt started doing it, it caught on fast. Soon, celebrities were doing it and everyone was trying it for size. When Bolt does it before a race, it's like he's saying: 'I am here and I'm the fastest. I've beaten you all before the race has even begun!' The crowds love it and Bolt has made it his own sign of success. Try doing the pose. I bet it makes you feel confident!

'I know what I can do, so I never doubt myself.'
USAIN BOLT

⇒ TAKE YOUR SPACE ⇐

You can create your own version of the Lightning Bolt by doing something called power posing. You can use this technique before an event that makes you feel nervous, like a school play or class speech.

Here's how to do it:

⚡ Stand as tall as you can, your hands on your hips and feet apart – like a superhero!

⚡ Throw your arms into the air or out by your side, whatever makes you feel as though you're taking up as much space in the world as you possibly can (but be careful not to whack them on the walls if you're in a tight space!)

⚡ Take a deep breath and let that air go right inside you. Blow it out through your mouth and do it again.

⚡ Hold the pose for as long as it takes to make you feel in control (of yourself, not the world – you're not a supervillain!).

That's it!

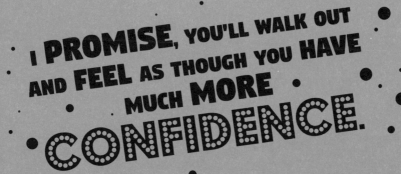

I PROMISE, YOU'LL WALK OUT AND FEEL AS THOUGH YOU HAVE MUCH MORE CONFIDENCE.

GAME CHANGERS

At the Women's Football World Cup held in France in 2019, an undeniable sporting **SUPERSTAR** took the tournament (and the world!) by storm.

Megan Rapinoe oozed confidence.

With her unmatchable ball skills, short, purple-tinted hair and habit of splaying her arms in a glorious celebration of victory when she scored a goal, Megan Rapinoe became the centrepiece of the tournament.

WHY?

It was because she believed in herself. And it showed. She also believed in her teammates and wasn't afraid to shower praise on them.

She is bold, she is outspoken, and she doesn't worry about criticism or 'falling off'. Her only concern is the positive impact she can have.

WHICH MEANS SHE ...

- ✶ can score goals under pressure
- ✶ is able to lead by example
- ✶ can stop opposing players in their tracks
- ✶ speaks up for girls and women
- ✶ has a positive team mentality
- ✶ believes she deserves her success

Megan Rapinoe is an inspirational person who uses her profile and her platform to speak out on behalf of those who do not have a voice. For anyone doubting themselves ...

that could be you, too.

'I don't think anyone who has ever spoken out, or stood up or had a brave moment, has regretted it. It's empowering and confidence-building and inspiring. Not only to other people, but to yourself.'

MEGAN RAPINOE

10 WAYS TO WEAR YOUR CLOAK OF CONFIDENCE

1 As soon as you wake up in the morning, pull your shoulders back, pop on your cloak of confidence, and wear it with pride!

2 Look outwards at the world, not just inwards at yourself. By that I mean look around you, be open-minded and try to support other people by your actions and your behaviour.

3 Praise other people. Praising others shows confidence, and when you are part of a team or group it's good to show that you appreciate other people's efforts.

4 Focus on LISTENING to people and actually HEAR what they are saying. Everyone loves being listened to and will respond positively to you for it. Actively listening to others shows confidence.

5 Make eye contact with people you're talking to. Looking someone in the eye will make you appear more confident.

make eye contact

6 Start your day positively with a confidence-boosting mantra that you can remember and repeat often. Keep it short and simple, such as 'My confidence is growing day by day' or 'I believe in myself'!

7 Everyone makes them, so accept your mistakes, take responsibility for them – and then move on!

8 Whatever happens, don't compare yourself to other people because ...

YOU ARE UNIQUE!

9 Recognise when someone is trying to support you, champion you or pay you a compliment. Let them!

10 Be brave, be bold. Put yourself out there, try something new – and whatever you do, don't be afraid of falling off!

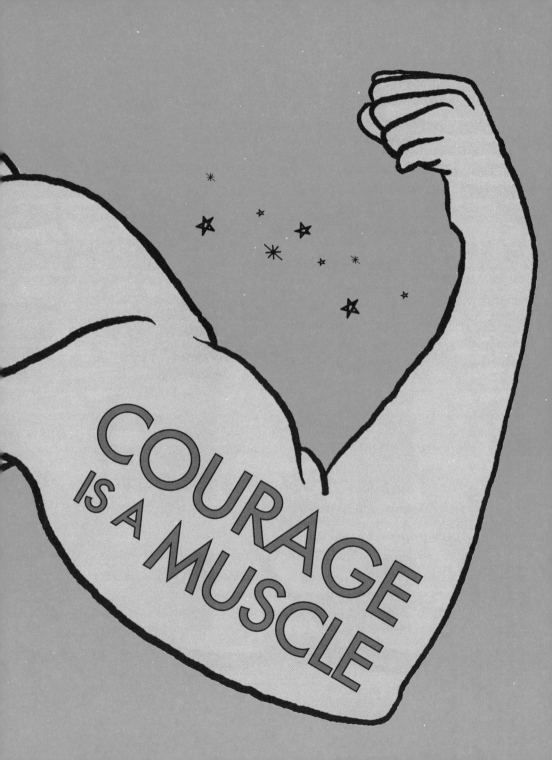

4

"You don't have to be a fantastic hero to do certain things, to compete. You can be just an ordinary chap, sufficiently motivated to reach challenging goals."

SIR EDMUND HILLARY,
EVEREST MOUNTAINEER AND EXPLORER

What does it mean to have courage?

Does it mean you have to:

Charge into a
BURNING BUILDING?

Take on a
roaring lion?

Pick up a
GIANT *spider?*

Swim with a shoal of
piranhas?

Erm. No.

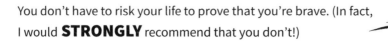

You don't have to risk your life to prove that you're brave. (In fact, I would **STRONGLY** recommend that you don't!)

Courage is personal. What scares YOU most? We all have our own fears. My mother is terrified of rats. Alice, my wife, is scared witless by spiders. For me, it's bats. One flew into my bedroom when I was very young and, to this day, I can still hear it squeaking round me as I hid under the bed covers. I was convinced it was a vampire bat trying to bite me. My dad came in and caught it in his cap so that he could put it back outside where it wanted to be.

It's important to be patient and understanding around each other's fears (to be honest, I shouldn't laugh at Alice being scared of spiders – sorry, Alice), but before we can help other people, we need to understand ourselves.

SO. TAKE A MINUTE.

What are the things that scare the pants off **you**?

Maybe it's:
- Standing up to give a speech
- Singing in front of other people
  (this has always been a big fear of mine)
- Swimming in the sea
- Starting a new school
- Making mistakes

But aside from singing to an audience, guess what is the thing that scares me the most?

OK, I'll tell you. It's being left out. And it all **started** when I was at school . . .

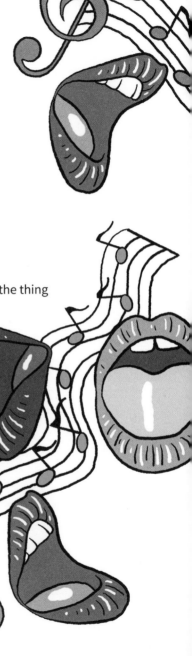

⇒ THINGS THAT GO BUMP ⇐
IN THE … SCHOOL?

When you were younger, you might have been scared of the dark or monsters hiding under your bed. As you get a bit older, the things that frighten you change. Once I turned 11 and then into my teens, the thing that I was most afraid of was being left out. Not being accepted in a group. Feeling like the **odd one out.**

The prospect of a new school term would terrify me. From day one, I worried about not fitting in. I hesitated before starting a conversation, waiting to see what other people said so that I could agree with them. I didn't follow fashion so I had no idea what the latest trend would be, and whatever I wore, I always seemed to get it wrong. Every other girl in my class seemed to have long hair when mine was short. And they *always* appeared to have the latest gadgets that I didn't, or were going on fancy summer holidays when I wasn't.

Like any of that matters, really. But it mattered to me then.

So I pretended.

Imagine for a moment the biggest, baggiest, oldest pair of pants that you own. Now, double them in size …

Yup. That's how big my pretending was. It was **BIG**.

Here's the truth. I was surrounded by people I thought were better than me, so in my desperation I decided to copy them.

How?

👍 **I never talked about my fears.** I just tried to fit in and pretended to be like everyone else.

👍 **I made up stories.** I'd pretend that I'd spent the summer somewhere other than at home, surrounded by animals. It's not that I wanted to be somewhere else – I loved being at home – but it didn't seem to be exciting enough.

👍 **I dreamed up things** I *wanted* to be or do just because I thought they would sound good to the other girls.

⋛ SO WHAT IS COURAGE? ⋚

The word *courage* comes from the Latin word *cor*, which means 'heart'. In Old French, as well, its meaning was connected to the heart and our innermost feelings.

There are so many different forms of courage.

Think of people who show courage in their everyday lives:

68

Yes, *you*.

Just as it takes courage to stand up for what you believe in and to help protect other people, it also takes courage to search for better ways of living – which is what you're doing right now. The first step is understanding that it's the *small* things we do every day that make the difference. You already have courage deep inside you. You just need to help it grow!

Try this:
- Clench your fist
- Stretch your arm out
- Bend it towards you
- Feel the bicep muscle in your upper arm tighten

If you did that EVERY DAY your muscle would get **stronger** and **BIGGER**, RIGHT?

But HOW do we build our 'COURAGE MUSCLE'?

Here's an exercise to help you.

It's called **'visualisation'**.

Lots of people in sport, on TV, or in business use it before they play a match, go live on air, or host a big meeting. Visualisation is all about painting positive mental 'pictures' of things in your mind before they happen. That way, when the same thing happens in real life you will be ready, as you've already 'seen' it happen successfully in your mind!

(1) Sit in a comfortable chair or lie down on the floor

(2) Spread your limbs out like a starfish and relax

(3) Close your eyes

(4) Think of the thing that scares you the most; it might be sky-diving, auditioning for *The X Factor* or picking up a spider

(5) Say out loud what you want to say in that situation

(6) Imagine doing it now with your best friend and really enjoying it!

(7) Open your eyes and laugh

(8) Repeat whenever you need to build your muscle of courage before doing something that scares you

Very soon you'll be able to throw away your big old Pretending Pants!

GAME CHANGERS

Bethany Hamilton is a world-class surfer. When she was 13 years old, Bethany was attacked by a tiger shark while surfing in Hawaii. It wrenched her left arm off at the shoulder.

SCARY, EH? MOST OF US WOULDN'T WANT TO GO NEAR THE SEA AGAIN – EVER!

But once she'd healed, Bethany was back in the water within a month. Two years later, she'd won her first US national surfing competition.

None of this meant that she wasn't scared. But she loved surfing more than anything, and not even a vicious shark attack was going to stop her trying to get back to her best. She learned to balance and control the board in her own style and has never once seen her new body as having an arm missing or lost.

Bethany's only ever seen it as a new challenge, which goes to show what a courageous mindset can do.

'COURAGE DOESN'T MEAN YOU DON'T GET AFRAID. COURAGE MEANS YOU DON'T LET FEAR STOP YOU.'

BETHANY HAMILTON, WORLD-CLASS SURFER

≳ SWIMMING INTO STRENGTH ≲

Adam Peaty is one of the best swimmers in the world. He is the Olympic champion for 100-metre breaststroke, a multiple world champion and the world record holder over 50 metres and 100 metres. And yet, do you know the thing that Adam Peaty was most afraid of when he was little?

You guessed it: **<u>WATER.</u>**

He loathed swimming lessons and at home, he wouldn't even sit down in the bath because he didn't trust the water. (His brothers had told him that sharks could swim up through the plughole so, not surprisingly, he was terrified.) His mum really didn't like taking him swimming because he screamed at the prospect of getting into the water, so she asked a friend to take him instead! When he realised that sharks couldn't attack him in the bath or in the local swimming pool, he started having fun with friends. He says he got into swimming rather than other sports because he realised it was something he was actually very good at – once he'd found his courage.

All it takes are baby strokes in the water. Or baby steps.

⋛ STICKING UP FOR PEOPLE ⋚

Courage isn't just about doing things for yourself. It's about sticking up for other people. Sometimes you might see someone being bullied or picked on. How often have you stayed silent or pretended you didn't notice something and then wished, moments later, you'd spoken up?

That's when you can help.

Sticking up for people isn't easy. It takes guts (another word for 'courage') and it also takes diplomacy (the ability to speak kindly).

Here are some tips:
- Choose your words carefully (see opposite page)
- Try to see both sides
- Encourage people on both sides to take a deep breath
- Ask them why they disagree
- Encourage each person to take a turn to speak
- Treat everyone with the same respect regardless of what you think
- Don't use name-calling. EVER.
- Let your friends know how they are making other people feel

DON'T SAY

I hate you!

DO SAY

Why don't we sit down and talk about this?

DON'T SAY

I just don't see the point of talking to you!

DO SAY

Can you help me understand?

DON'T SAY

Why don't you both just shut up!

DO SAY

Why don't you speak first?

Then, we'll listen to the other person.

It's not easy to come up with the right words at the right time. Practise by thinking about what you could say if you get in that situation.

When I was at primary school I was being picked on by a boy. He kept on and on saying hurtful things and being unkind. I got more and more wound up and eventually, I lost my temper and shouted at him. I said things back to him that were just as bad as what he'd said to me.

Did I feel good about myself?

No.

Afterwards, I thought of all the ways I could have responded better.

I started to jot down helpful phrases that I could use to defend myself or someone else:
- ✶ I'm sorry that you feel you need to behave this way
- ✶ Is there anything I can do to help?
- ✶ Why would you be so unkind?
- ✶ You probably didn't mean to be that rude

I practised saying them so that if I was in a situation where I needed to react, I wouldn't have to think too long about it. Try it now and think of some of your own. The main thing is not to be mean and to try to keep the tone light. Of course, you don't want to start a fight but you DO want to be able to support yourself or someone who needs it.

Sometimes you don't even have to say *anything* – you can walk away or put your arm around someone else and help *them* walk away. To walk away can take more courage than anything.

But most important of all in these situations, remember that you should always ask for help from an adult if things get serious.

So look around you. Be aware of other people and be prepared to stand up for them if needs be.

That takes real courage, but you've been practising, so you can do it.

COURAGE is a mUSCle

STEP OUT OF YOUR COMFORT ZONE

I work on live TV, which is fun, but what people don't see is that I have to summon up all of my courage before going on set. Live TV shows such as Wimbledon or the Olympics can be very unpredictable and things are always going wrong.

So here is my recipe for courage when I'm presenting live. OK, this may not be something you're planning on doing any time soon, but perhaps there are some take-aways ...

COMFORT
ZONE

✴ Firstly, I do lots of 'homework' (which involves reading and making notes) to ensure I'm as prepared as possible for the show

✴ I imagine various outcomes of what might happen and talk through them in my head so that I am sharp and confident about what I am saying or doing

✴ I think about all the people who are supporting me – family, friends, my colleagues – and this makes me smile and feel more relaxed

✴ When I see the red light on the camera that signifies we're 'Live On Air', I know that I need to just go with it and do the best I can

✴ I know that if I'm feeling nervous, it's because I care; the nerves are a reward for doing something I love

✴ That's the thing about having the courage to do things that scare you:

ONCE YOU TAKE THE LEAP AND LEARN TO ENJOY BEING OUT OF YOUR COMFORT ZONE, IT'S THE BEST AND MOST MEMORABLE EXPERIENCE OF ALL.

5

'*You can't use up creativity. The more you use, the more you have.*'

MAYA ANGELOU

Once upon a time, I was told that there's no such thing as a *bad* idea. But when my brother Andrew and I were little, we came up with a lot of bad ideas … starting with the time that we painted the puppy shed a lovely shade of cornflower blue.

I know.

Bear with me, I'll explain.

At the time, we had a boxer dog. Candy was my best friend – big eyes, slobbery kisses and unending loyalty. Plus, she was about to have puppies (one of which was Flossy, the dog I taught to do a high-five!). Dogs like to have a nest when they're about to give birth, and we had lots of dogs in our family, so we set about converting an old shed into a special retreat for Candy and her puppies. It was perfect. That was until my brother and I got creative with an old tin of paint ...

Yes, we gave the puppy shed a proper makeover. We painted the door, the roof, the walls – and we painted each other, top to toe in cornflower blue. We were having fun and got carried away. What had started as the perfect home for a family of puppies had become a bit of a mess.

Our creativity had spilled over into chaos.

Mum and dad weren't thrilled. Fortunately, Candy's labour went well and the five squirming little puppies distracted them from our bad idea.

No harm done!

But Andrew and I learned a lesson that day. Try not to spoil a fantastically creative idea by doing the job badly.

⋛YOUR LIGHTBULB MOMENT!⋚

What's the most **brilliant** idea you've ever had?

It might be any of the below.

Can you spot which one was MY brilliant idea?

1. A charity challenge you thought of to raise money
2. A costume you came up with for World Book Day
3. Eating sausages and marmalade on toast
4. A story you wrote or a painting you made
5. A unique game that you came up with for your family

Answer:

3. It's true! I liked to eat sausages with toast and marmalade. Together, at the same time – the sausages lying along the top. It's delicious, I promise. I came up with this creative solution to breakfast when I got a bit fed up with eating the same old cereal every single day.

We also (very gently and kindly) once dressed up our dogs with capes and hats, and pretended they were characters from history. Cindy the lurcher was Elizabeth I. She looked a bit terrifying with her long nose and big eyes framed by a bonnet, but she loved it **(I think)**.

85

Your imagination is amazing.

It can take you anywhere at any time and its power is endless. Think of each idea as a spark of light. A light bulb switching on, or a firework going off. Every time you have an idea, write it down in a special notebook so that you don't forget. You will end up with loads of bright 'lightbulb moments', some more useful than others (and probably more useful than mine!), but all of them precious.

'GOOD IDEAS CAN COME AT ANY TIME, SO ALWAYS HAVE A PENCIL TO HAND.'

JAMES DYSON, INVENTOR AND ENTREPRENEUR

⇒EARLY DREAMS⇐

My careers teacher at school thought I wanted to be an inventor. She asked us in class one day what we all wanted to be when we grew up. My hand shot up in the air.

'An eventer!'

I shouted out. I was certain that's what I wanted in life.

'Oh, that's interesting,' said Mrs T. 'What do you want to *invent*?'

'Not an IN-ventor,' I explained. 'An E-venter. A three-day-eventer. It's a rider. You know – like a triathlon, but on a horse. I want to go to the Olympics.'

She gave me the sort of stare that my father used to give the dogs when they'd let off a bad smell. Mrs T was not impressed. She moved on to the next girl in class, who wanted to be a lawyer.

I bet it's happened to you, too. You've told someone that you want to be a footballer and they've laughed. Or you say you want to be the lead singer in a band and they snort. I should have realised that my ambitions were a little unusual compared to others. Not everyone grows up surrounded by horses and wants to ride them every single day of their life, forever. I count myself really lucky that I did.

This wouldn't be the last time that I would understand that my dreams were special to me, but it was the first time.

> *Your dreams are special to you as well.*

Not everyone will understand them or encourage you to follow them, but don't let that stop you following your own path.

As it turns out, I did go to the Olympics, but not as a competitor. But if I HAD grown up to be an inventor, I would have tried to come up with a way to travel without harming the environment.

Like a **flying machine**
that runs on solar power.

Who knows? One day someone might make that happen.

And it might be **you**!

⋝ THE 10-METRE CHALLENGE ⋜

I want you – yes, **you**, reading this book – to use your creativity to change the world. OK, that's a big ask. So let's scale that down a bit. How about using your creativity to change the 10 metres around you …

(1) **Think about the 10 metres around you – at school, at home, at your grandparents' house, at your club, with your friends**

(2) **Who is in your 10-metre radius?**

(3) **Have a think about how you could possibly use your creativity to improve things for you and for them? Write them down, brainstorm them, draw them, build them, paint them, sew them, model them or knit them!**

(4) **Is there anyone who can help you achieve these things?**

(5) **Think about how you can encourage your friends to come up with ideas to improve your 10 metres, too. After all, the more voices, the better.**

This is a chance to shout your (and your friends') ideas from the rooftops! I want to encourage you, and those in your 10 metres, to be brave enough to say what they think, suggest alternative solutions, encourage inventive and different ways of solving some of the problems we face in our everyday life.

⇒ ARE WE BORN CREATIVE? ⇐

Well, if you look at the life of **Leonardo da Vinci**, I'd say yes!

He was the great Italian artist, architect and engineer of the Renaissance period who painted the Mona Lisa and who is considered as one of the greatest artists of all time. Leonardo drew early designs for the helicopter and the parachute. Yet he never went to school. He taught himself to read, write and paint. But nobody taught him how to be creative,

the seed of creativity was inside him all along.

Leonardo surrounded himself with interesting people and was incredibly curious.

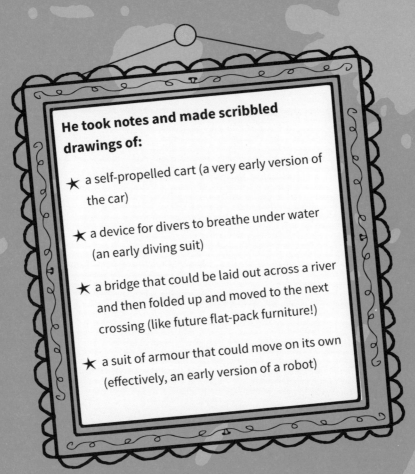

He took notes and made scribbled drawings of:

★ a self-propelled cart (a very early version of the car)

★ a device for divers to breathe under water (an early diving suit)

★ a bridge that could be laid out across a river and then folded up and moved to the next crossing (like future flat-pack furniture!)

★ a suit of armour that could move on its own (effectively, an early version of a robot)

Leonardo da Vinci was the most creative person in an age of creativity, but he didn't have access to education or the internet. Just imagine that.

This means that you could achieve even more than Leonardo da Vinci!

NO PRESSURE!

THE WORLD'S BIGGEST PE LESSON

In March 2020, as the announcement was made that we should all stay at home, Joe Wicks offered free fitness classes every morning. So every day at 9am for 13 weeks he was there, inspiring kids around the world to join in. His classes, called *PE With Joe*, had 70 million views worldwide from Russia to Ireland, Australia to Germany, and broke the record for the number of people watching live on YouTube.

Joe became the world's favourite PE teacher!

You may have joined in, doing star jumps, climbing a 'ladder' or running on the spot. He had a dream of getting kids to exercise every morning and he made it happen. Joe kept it fun by playing daft games and dressing up for Fancy Dress Fridays, but his basic message stayed the same:

Exercise is GOOD for us!

If we can all do something every day that gets us active, our brains will work better and we'll be happier! Joe's was a simple but creative idea that helped him raise **£500,000** for charity.

M IS FOR MOBOT

The London Olympics and Paralympics of 2012 was the greatest and most enjoyable summer of my life, and a time when we all felt positive and inspired.

One of the stars of the Olympics for Team GB was the distance runner Mo Farah (now Sir Mo). He won gold medals in the 5,000 and 10,000 metres and I bet you remember his celebration?

Yep.

He put his two hands over his head to create the shape of an M.

Do you know who came up with that idea?

Well, it may be my only claim to creativity – **but I did!** So how did I help an international sports superstar with his own personal 'brand'?

I appeared on a TV show where we were challenged to come up with a victory pose for Mo Farah (imagine Usain's 'Lightning Bolt' or Megan Rapinoe's victory stance). We wanted something that everyone would remember. All of a sudden, my brain sparked into life.

THIS WAS FUN!

I allowed my mind to freewheel and remembered a favourite song from when I was a child.

'I know! I know!'

I shouted out. I was really excited.

'He could do the M! The M from "YMCA"!'

If you haven't heard it before, *'YMCA'* is a famous song where the singers, The Village People, used to act out the letters above their heads as they sang. The M was easy – just a bend in each arm with your fingers touching your head and you've got it.

As soon as I suggested it, I felt a bit silly. That can happen sometimes when you suggest an idea. Unless other people support you, it's really scary.

I blushed with embarrassment.

Then I heard the presenter, James Corden, say:

'That's a great idea.
We can call it THE MOBOT!'

Mo tried it out and he liked it because it was _fun_.

The audience joined in and everyone agreed it felt right. Mo starting using the move and, after he won in London, he did the Mobot on the podium. And after that, Mo began to use this victory sign every time he won a race.

What seemed like a daft idea became real.

THAT'S THE POWER OF CREATIVITY.

THE SHOWER OF INSPIRATION

Shhhh ... here is my super-secret tip for finding your creativity that doesn't involve you having to sit in front of a computer or a notebook. Because, what I've found is that creativity appears when you're least expecting it – usually when you are doing something meditative that doesn't require a lot of thought or concentration, or something that takes you outside of your normal way of thinking.

When you are feeling like this your brain can suddenly change gear, and ...

POW!

You have a great creative idea.

So, my secret tip is ... wait for it ...
I have my best ideas

IN THE SHOWER.

It's true!

I turn my shower to freezing cold for the last minute or so. It's quite a shock to the system, I can tell you, but it leaves you tingling, refreshed and sends the blood pumping through your body. For some reason this sensation activates my brain and suddenly ideas are popping like light bulbs all over the place. Give it a go!

But if you don't fancy an ice-cold shower, then exercise such as walking, cycling, running, or focused activities like colouring, painting, doodling, knitting or sewing are all great to get your creative ideas flowing, too!

6

'When the whole world is silent, even one voice is powerful.'

MALALA YOUSAFZAI

If you could say anything you wanted – something really important – **what would it be?**

CAN I HAVE A BISCUIT?

is not the answer I was after …

What I mean is, if you felt really strongly, really **passionately** about something, how would you get your message across?

✦ **Have a think about something that really matters to you?**

- 👍 Standing up against cruelty to animals
- 👍 Protesting against climate change
- 👍 Protecting our oceans from plastic pollution
- 👍 Fighting racism
- 👍 Supporting the rights of LGBTQ+ people
- 👍 Supporting equal rights for everyone!

There are lots of ways of showing your support by standing up and speaking out. And sometimes a small voice or action becomes much bigger. One person or group marching can become thousands or millions speaking up in support of the Black Lives Matter movement. Or one schoolgirl can mobilise schoolchildren all around the world to go on strike as a protest against climate change.

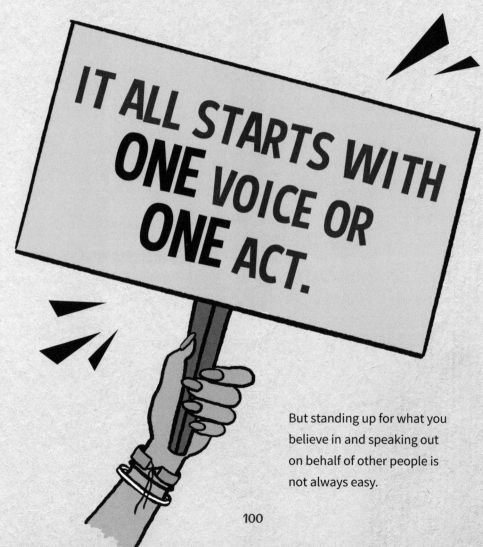

IT ALL STARTS WITH ONE VOICE OR ONE ACT.

But standing up for what you believe in and speaking out on behalf of other people is not always easy.

≳ FINDING MY VOICE ≲

In all honesty, it took me a while to *find my voice* and that goes for when I was a child, as well as being an adult (more on this later in the chapter).

Looking back, I can think of loads of times when I wish I'd stuck up for someone who was being picked on at school, or wish I'd kicked back against my parents' view of the world. From when I was really young, I cared deeply about the rights of girls and women, mainly because my dad just couldn't understand what the problem was. He'd grown up in a completely different time and didn't see why it mattered so much if women didn't get paid as much as men, or if they were judged by how they looked rather than what they knew.

When I tried to argue my case about equal rights for girls and women, my parents were just a bit baffled and tried to laugh it off. My grandmother thought the word 'feminist' was a swear word and wouldn't let me use it, and even when we had our first female prime minister back in 1979, my father said it would take him a while 'to get used to a woman running the country'. This from a man who trained racehorses for the Queen!

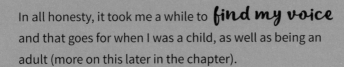

As you can see, it was a tricky time for me as a young equal rights campaigner.

The adults around me seemed to think that women couldn't do things just because they were, well, women. I had the opposite view and thought there were plenty of jobs we could do just as well as, if not better than, men – if we were given the chance.

Since that time, I have continued to passionately support equal pay and opportunities for women and girls, and championed women's sport, as I think it's a really important way in which women are seen differently. On the sports field, girls and women can be strong and competitive and ambitious. These issues really matter to me, so I am prepared to stand up and speak out for them,

in the HOPE that I can help bring about some CHANGE.

⇒ GRETA SPEAKS OUT ⇐

When I was growing up, it was generally accepted that adults knew what they were doing (even if I didn't agree with them) and children had to listen and follow their example. It's not that way now and that's partly because of a young girl from Sweden called **Greta Thunberg**. She ignored the old rules of following what the adults said and decided to

STAND UP AND SPEAK OUT IN HER OWN WAY.

Greta's message is that **climate change** is the greatest danger to our existence and that political leaders have not been doing enough to tackle the causes of pollution and global warming. By way of protest, she sat outside the Swedish Parliament building with a homemade sign every Friday. Pretty soon, the world started to take notice. School kids all around the world started to strike and organise marches of their own.

Greta spoke at the UN Climate Action Summit in 2019 and has become an iconic figure in the climate change movement because, despite her youth, her inexperience and her lack of political power, she made her voice heard. But Greta is not the only young person speaking up about things that matter.

Coco Gauff is one of the youngest players on the professional Women's Tennis Association Tour – but that doesn't stop her being one of the most **powerful and inspiring.**

Coco made a big impact playing her first Grand Slam tournament in 2019 at just 15 years old. Thousands flocked to see her matches at Wimbledon and the US Open, and millions more watched on TV. But away from the tennis court, she is determined to **use her voice.** At a Black Lives Matter protest rally in Florida, in the summer of 2020, she gave a rousing speech to the crowd, with no notes and not a hint of nerves. Coco urged everyone to stand up and speak out, no matter how big or small their reach.

Coco knows that her rising profile in sport means she is recognised and that if she speaks, people will listen. She certainly does not see being a teenager as a barrier and is inspired that younger people are leading movements around the world. As Coco says:

> **'My generation has just decided it was time to speak up on our own about things.'**

This is your
generation.

You are **never** too young to stand up and speak out.

GAME CHANGERS

Marcus Rashford, the Manchester United and England striker, has helped raise over £20 million to provide food for the children of low-income families. In 2020, when he found out that the government wouldn't be providing vouchers for free school meals over the summer holidays, Marcus wrote an open letter to all MPs asking them to change their mind. He pointed out how much these kids needed healthy food and that they wouldn't get it without the vouchers.

Rashford then used his social media channels to highlight the difficulties facing families who were not earning loads of money. He spoke honestly about how his own experience growing up had made him determined to help others in that situation. As a result of his actions, school meals vouchers were reinstated for 1.3 million children.

HIS VOICE MADE ALL THE DIFFERENCE.

Quarterback **Colin Kaepernick**'s name is not associated so much with the game of American Football these days as with his simple act of defiance that has generated press all over the world. Seeing more and more incidents of police brutality towards black people, Kaepernick felt he had to stand up (or in this case, kneel down) and do something.

In 2016, as his teammates stood with their hands on their hearts to salute the US flag while the national anthem played, Kaepernick would sit down or 'take the knee' in the crowded stadium. Though many disagreed with him, he never stopped kneeling, and now sportspeople and others in all walks of life use his 'stance' to protest against injustice.

Kaepernick knelt down rather than stood up, and he used a gesture rather than his words, but it was hugely powerful.

HE SHOWED THE WAY.

SPEAKING OUT AND ME

I didn't enjoy my early days at school because, for a long time, I didn't feel like I fitted in. I was too scared to say anything at all, let alone speak up on something important, like supporting equal rights for everyone. I didn't think I would be listened to and so I said

nothing.

I didn't realise that if you say nothing, you are, in a way, saying you agree with the way things are. If you don't agree with what's going on, you have to find a way of saying so, or at least of suggesting an alternative.

As an adult, I also took a while to feel really comfortable in my own skin — and especially in regard to relationships.

You see, I was brought up to think that the only 'acceptable' relationship meant being married to a man with a big wedding in a church. I was worried that if people discovered that I was in a relationship with a woman it would mean that I got teased, insulted or even that I might be discriminated against when it came to choosing presenters for big events and programmes on TV.

A lot has changed in the world since then, *thankfully*.

> *Love is the most precious thing to be celebrated and whether you love a man or a woman, it really doesn't matter.*

The most important thing is to cherish and protect that love, which is what I've tried to do. I am so proud and happy that Alice is my wife.

I think about how much **stress** I suffered throughout the years when I knew that I was gay, but I didn't think it was something I could stand up and speak out about without negative judgement from others. But, believe me, the fear of how you imagine people will react to you speaking out is often much worse than the reality. My parents didn't reject me, and most other people were really **kind** and **supportive**. I knew I couldn't control what others thought about me, anyway, so I learned not to care.

I REFUSE TO LIVE MY LIFE ACCORDING TO WHAT GOSSIPS MIGHT SAY.

Whatever it is that you face in life that you feel ashamed about or that you don't feel you can share, I promise you, it will be better when you do. In being open and honest – in standing up and speaking out for what I believed in – I became so much happier, and therefore, *nicer* as a person.

By speaking out for myself, it also meant that I could speak up for the causes that I believe in. Whether it's equal pay, equal rights, mental health or animal welfare, I can try to offer support for those who need it, and question those in authority who don't understand what they're doing wrong.

10 WAYS TO SPEAK OUT WITH CONFIDENCE

Whether you are speaking or presenting to your class or to a bigger group, here are some of the tips I've learned in my career which help me to speak confidently to anyone, from small groups to audiences of millions on live TV!

1. Plan ahead.

If you are presenting a topic to a group or your class, have a clear idea of what you want to say and why. Make sure you've had at least two run-throughs out loud, so that you're really comfortable and familiar with your material. I prefer to use bullet points rather than a fully written-out speech or presentation because it allows me more freedom to improvise and sounds more 'natural'.

2. Take it steady.

Wait a full 2 seconds before you start speaking. And during your presentation or while you are talking, don't be afraid to pause. Silence and pauses can be really clever ways of making people *listen*. Pausing while speaking also communicates confidence.

3 **Check your posture.**

Stand up (or sit up) as straight as you can. Keep your head high and your shoulders back. I always feel more empowered when I'm standing up (you'll see I often stand up when I can on live TV!). It makes me feel more energised and helps my breathing.

4 **And speaking of which – don't forget to breathe!**

When I'm presenting on TV I always try to take a big, deep breath into my belly, and then breathe out through my nose rather than through my mouth. Breathing through your mouth can make you sound a bit breathless and anxious. Try breathing through your nose, it's really worth it.

SMILE!

5 **Say it with a smile.**

Smiling can project warmth and feeling into your voice, and affects how you speak and how other people respond to what you're saying. I always try to smile (or even just think about smiling) while I'm interviewing people. I think it helps bring out the best in them.

6 **Stay calm and focused.**

Even if you're speaking about a topic that is very close to your heart, try not to get worked up. It doesn't help people to understand your point if you show anger or frustration (believe me, I know!)

7 **Body talk.**

Try to keep your body language 'open', and use your hands to convey excitement and confidence about what you are saying. Avoid folding your arms, fiddling with your hair or touching your face, as these things can make you seem nervous.

CONFIDENCE

anger

8 **Look into my eyes!**
Make *eye contact* with the people you are speaking to, it makes you seem much more confident about what you are saying.

9

DRINK WATER!

I always have a glass or bottle of water to hand before I go on TV or on stage. Being hydrated helps you think more clearly, but also helps your mouth to not dry up mid-sentence.

10 **Be polite.**
If you are making a presentation or speaking to a group, thank them for their time or for listening. It shows confidence and consideration. Also say '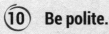*thank you*' at the end as a way of finishing what you've said.

IT WILL GIVE A POLITE FULL STOP TO YOUR SPEECH.

BE BENDY AND STRETCH YOURSELF!

7

'Just try new things. Don't be afraid.
Step out of your comfort zones and soar.'

MICHELLE OBAMA, AUTHOR,
SPEAKER AND FORMER
FIRST LADY OF THE UNITED STATES

When I was busy falling off **on purpose** at the age of 9 (see Chapter 1 if you need a refresher on that), it didn't occur to me for one moment that I might get hurt. And even when I broke my collarbone falling off (by accident) as a toddler, it didn't take long to mend because when we're young, our bones are very soft and bendy. It's only when we get a bit older that our bones become harder, and less easy to mend themselves.

I think this can be true of our brains.

If we can train our brains to be bendy, flexible and adaptable, then surely we can turn our minds to **all sorts of things**?

As I've said before, when I was at school I thought I had to look a certain way (mainly wear baggy jumpers, skinny jeans and have long, flowing hair). I thought I had to know all the words to the latest hit songs, and that I should try to impress boys all the time.

The other girls talked about clothes and make-up and stuff they wanted to have. If they looked into the future, they talked about having big houses and loads of children. Some wanted to work as fashion models, actresses or singers. Some wanted to be doctors or lawyers, but none of us really understood what it meant. Everyone, including me, said what they thought their parents or their teachers *wanted to hear.*

I found it all a bit boring and it didn't make sense to me. Trouble was, I didn't have much idea *what* I wanted to be, but it didn't involve wearing fancy clothes. I didn't want to follow the same path as everyone else, I just wasn't sure if there was a path that would take me where I **wanted** to go. My brother Andrew knew what he wanted to do – the same thing as our dad, two uncles and both grandfathers.

HE WOULD TRAIN RACEHORSES.

There was no great plan for me. So I had to make up one for myself – which, to be honest, was great because I got to choose, and when I started writing for newspapers and working on the radio, I felt as if I was doing something really *exciting*, a bit scary and, most important, a job no one else in my family had ever done before. I also knew that I wanted **variety** and **flexibility** in my life.

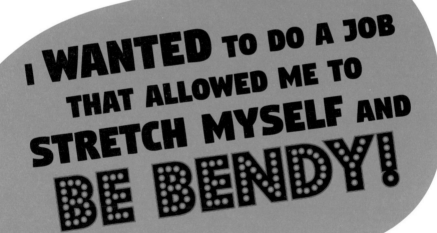

I WANTED TO DO A JOB THAT ALLOWED ME TO STRETCH MYSELF AND BE BENDY!

SHAPESHIFTERS

I absolutely love my pets, of course, but I'm also truly fascinated by the ways that different animals can flex, stretch and adapt to their surroundings.

Did you know that some animals really can shape shift? The **chameleon** is the headline act in this scenario as it can famously change colour to signal to other chameleons, but did you know that a few animals can morph into something else entirely –

usually to fool anything that might want to eat them.

The **tiny, mutable rainfrog**, found in the forests of Ecuador, can transform itself in a matter of seconds from having a spiky, spiny texture on its outer skin to being smooth and glossy.

120

DON'T EAT ME!

The **pufferfish**, as the name suggests, can puff itself up like a balloon by filling its stomach with air or water. Who wants to eat a giant ball of spikes? The **mimic octopus** changes its colour to camouflage itself, but can also imitate other types of fish. By sweeping its legs backwards into a streamlined shape it can look like a flatfish gliding over the ocean floor. Or it can use one leg to pretend to be a sea snake. Quite brilliant. And, don't forget, of course, the **butterfly**, which has one of the most incredible transformations of all. It has always amazed me that a hairy little wriggler can turn into that beautiful, brightly coloured creature with patterned wings, floating through the flowers.

Films and books are full of ordinary people who transform themselves into superheroes – Peter Parker into Spiderman, Bruce Banner into the Incredible Hulk, Clark Kent into Superman, Carol Danvers into Captain Marvel. But fear not, I'm not suggesting for a minute that we should all be shapeshifters or superheroes!

MY POINT IS THAT WE CAN ALL FLEX, STRETCH AND ADAPT OURSELVES WHEN WE HAVE TO, OR WHEN WE WANT TO.

Everything and anything **is** possible. The only thing stopping us, most of the time, is

US.

So, close your eyes for a minute and imagine what you could do. Let your imagination run wild. What if you could learn to do something that no one in your family has done before or that no one in your school has ever tried?

Could you:

BOG SNORKEL
(this is a thing)

Breakdance

Climb a
mountain

Yodel

BECOME *fluent* **IN ITALIAN OR MANDARIN**

Play
the bagpipes

GO WILD SWIMMING

Most people end up doing the same old stuff because it's what everyone else is doing. They play the same sports, wear the same clothes, listen to the same music, have the same hairstyle.

Once in a while you might get the chance to do something really **different**, something you never thought you could do. Wouldn't it be cool to stretch yourself, and say **'Yes, please!'**

You never know, you might be <u>REALLY</u> good at it.

⋛ PEOPLE WHO PIVOT ⋚

Do you play netball or basketball? Pivoting is a technique that is used in both of these sports to be able to stop and change direction quickly.

But people can 'pivot' in lots of other areas of life, too. Pivoting means the ability to be **flexible**, to be **adaptable**, to be **stretchy, bendy** – and open to new ideas and experiences.

Michelle Obama has flexed and stretched throughout her life. She's been a lawyer, a fundraiser, a mother, the First Lady of the United States, a bestselling author and a public speaker. When she started her first job as a lawyer, she thought she had to stay on one track, stick to the path she had chosen and follow it precisely.

DO YOU EVER GET THAT FEELING WHEN YOU'RE GOING SOMEWHERE AND YOU KNOW YOU'VE TAKEN THE WRONG TURN?

DO YOU STOP AND RETRACE YOUR STEPS, OR DO YOU CARRY ON REGARDLESS, HOPING YOU'LL GET THERE IN THE END?

When I'm hiking or walking (both big passions of mine), I am a shocker for trying to carry on in the direction that I *think* is right. Often I've got lost because I refuse to stop and look at a map. Thankfully, technology now comes to the rescue and GPS has helped me no end.

Anyway, back to our Michelle story ... a great friend of hers died very young and, not long afterwards, so did Michelle's father. It forced her to look at her own life and appreciate how **precious** it was. At around the same time she met Barack Obama and fell in love. She began writing down her thoughts in a diary and it was when she saw it all on the page that she had a

LIGHTBULB MOMENT!

Suddenly she realised that she didn't enjoy working in the legal profession. She was doing it because she thought it was the sensible option and that it was the natural step for someone who was moving up the ladder, but it didn't give her fulfilment or satisfaction.

She gave herself permission to change track and went to work for the Mayor of Chicago, so that she could have an **impact** on things that really mattered to people in their everyday lives.

Michelle was willing to bend, to be flexible, to experiment, and is now one of the most influential and important women in the world.

When the champion boxer **Nicola Adams** was 12 years old, her life changed course …

The babysitter had cancelled, so her mum took Nicola and her brother along with her to an aerobics class. It was at a boxing gym, full of boys and men punching bags and training. Nicola wanted to give it a go. She enjoyed it and signed up to regular boxing classes.

It was an accident, a fluke that she had gone to the gym at all, but if she hadn't been **flexible** in her mind, if she hadn't **pivoted** and been prepared to do something totally different, Nicola Adams would not have become the

FIRST female boxer in the world to win an Olympic gold medal.

Didier Drogba was a brilliant footballer, and played for clubs all over the world. When he retired he became a Goodwill Ambassador for the United Nations Development Programme. He has been credited with helping to bring **peace** to his home country, the Ivory Coast, after five years of civil war.

Did you know that **Vera Wang**, the famous fashion designer, started out as a figure skater? She pivoted into journalism and worked for *Vogue* magazine for 15 years. When she was due to get married, she realised how difficult it was to find a stylish wedding dress, so she designed her own. She opened her first boutique in New York City a year later.

Dwayne 'The Rock' Johnson was a professional wrestler for eight years before he became an actor and found fame on the big screen, appearing in movies like *Moana* and the *Jumanji* films. The Rock has become one of the biggest box-office stars in the world.

YOUR ABILITY TO FLEX, ← STRETCH → AND ADAPT CAN CHANGE YOUR LIFE. MAKE BRAVE CHOICES.

⇒ BOUNCING BACK ⇐

The brilliant thing about being bendy is that it also helps you to cope with *'falling off and getting back on'*. It helps you to see that you can change your track, pivot, adapt, and try do something different that works better for you instead.

We all have setbacks; believe me, I know all about this. I've had loads.

When I wasn't picked as one of the main presenters for the Olympics in 2012, it was a real blow. I had hoped to be up in the main studio, fronting the coverage every evening. I was gutted. Then I realised that in order to bounce back, I had to think about and do things differently. So I 'reframed' my thinking so that I could see the negative as a positive. After all, I was still a part of the BBC presenting team and, even better, as a 'roving reporter', rather than being stuck in a studio all the time, I would be able to cover lots of different sports!

I decided to look at this 'failure' in a *positive* light, as a chance to do things *differently*. I chose to be bendy and it worked. I had the best time reporting on swimming, women's boxing, show-jumping and all sorts of other events. I could be in lots of different places seeing a variety of fascinating events and interviewing all sorts of interesting people.

I did a ton of 'homework', reading up on all the athletes and making sure I knew what they had done at previous competitions. (My notebooks and highlighter pens really came in useful, I can tell you!) I'd prepped so thoroughly that I was ready to talk about a subject for one minute or even 10 minutes if I had to. Learning all those facts meant I could be flexible and bendy in my presenting role and, what's more, I could really enjoy it.

> *It worked out for the best because I made that decision to flex, stretch and bend.*

So if this kind of setback affects you – for example, if you don't get the part in the school play that you were really hankering after, miss out on a place in the choir or football team, or get a disappointing score in a test – don't let your negative thoughts get the better of you. Being bendy and finding the positives in any situation can help us all **bounce** back.

BENDY BODY, BENDY MIND

Did you know that flexing, stretching and bending your body can actually help your mind? We're all so busy these days: school, clubs, hobbies, helping out at home (you do, don't you?) as well as things like keeping up with friends.

Phew! It's amazing that we can keep up with it all ...

So when things get a bit hectic for me, I calm myself down with a couple of simple, **bendy** exercises that work wonders. So grab a mat or towel and prepare to get flexible!

①   Flat out!
Stretch out flat on your mat or towel. Raise your arms above your head and point your feet. Feel your whole body stretch from your fingers down to your toes. Hold this posture and take 3 deep, relaxing breaths.

②   Stretch yourself.
Come to a cross-legged sitting position. Take your right arm and stretch it over your head towards your left ear. Lean your whole body towards

the left, using your left hand to support you. You should feel a nice stretch all the way down the right side of your body. Now repeat this movement on the other side, starting with your left arm.

③ Give your knees a hug.
Lie on your back and pull your knees into your chest. Breathe in deeply and let it out slowly. Then rock your body gently from side to side. This gives your back muscles a gentle stretch and massage.

④ Do the butterfly!
Sit on the floor. Bring the soles of your feet together in front of you, making your legs into the shape of butterfly wings. Breathe in as you lift your arms over your head. As you release your arms back down, breathe out.

⑤ Stand up tall.
Get back on your feet. Put your shoulders back and stand tall.

YOU SHOULD BE NICE AND FLEXIBLE AND GOOD TO GO!

8

'You can't be that kid standing at the top of the waterslide, overthinking it. You have to go down the chute.'

TINA FEY, ACTRESS AND WRITER

As I write this, I'm watching our newborn kittens. They are three days old, their eyes not open yet and their ears flat to their little heads. Their motivation is easy to work out – when they're hungry (which is about every 10 minutes) they want milk from their mother. When they're full, they want to sleep.

That's it.

That's their motivation.

They fight each other for their place at Button's tummy, blindly batting away with paws and claws. When they finally get the teat they want, they suck until they can't suck any more and fall asleep with their mouths still locked in place.

When you were a baby, your aims would have been pretty similar –

EAT, SLEEP, POOP, REPEAT.

But as you grew older, your goals probably grew with you: to make the perfect chocolate cake, learn how to skateboard, or do sign language.

Your motivation is what makes you want to do things, even if they're not easy.

It's what keeps you MOVING.

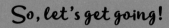

So, let's get going!

⋛ THE ART OF GETTING STARTED ⋚

I recently set myself the challenge of running to get fit.

I thought it would be so easy …

① Put on running kit
② Step outside
③ **Run!**

Often, it's more like …

① Put on running kit
② Step outside
③ Realise it's raining
④ Hurry back inside
⑤ Sit down on the sofa with a cup of tea

Resisting the urge to stop before you've even got going demands a little mental kick.

Sometimes I find it helps to have a few words with myself.

Words like ...

JUST PUT ONE FOOT IN FRONT OF THE OTHER, CLARE!

Sorry, Clare, making a cup of tea does NOT count as exercise

A chocolate biscuit is NOT one of your 5 a day

You'll feel **SO** much better when you've finished, Clare

Clare, remember that no one ever wished they hadn't gone for a **RUN!**

⇒ BROTHERS AND SISTERS ⇐

When I was little, my motivation was to beat my brother at everything. I wanted to do things *with* him, but I (mainly) wanted to do them **better** than him. If you have a brother or sister, you will know exactly what I mean.

> They can be so annoying and yet you can't imagine life without them.

Plenty of brothers and sisters drive each other on, and it can make both of them stronger and more successful. Think about the tennis stars Venus and Serena Williams, or Olympic triathletes Alistair and Jonny Brownlee. Peyton and Eli Manning both became hugely successful quarterbacks in American Football. Meanwhile, the Ukrainian boxing brothers, Vitali and Wladimir Klitschko, ruled heavyweight boxing for years.

NEXT TIME YOUR BROTHER OR SISTER STARTS WINDING YOU UP, THINK ABOUT **HOW** YOU COULD USE YOUR ENERGIES TO **MOTIVATE** EACH OTHER TO GET **BETTER** AT SOMETHING!

⋛ WHAT MOTIVATES YOU? ⋚

Everyone has different things that can light a fire under their bums, driving them on. These were some of mine growing up (and some still today), I wonder if yours are the same?

- **Trying to impress your parents**
- **Making teachers or coaches proud**
- **Proving something to people who doubt you**
- **Supporting teammates or friends**
- **Raising money for charity**
- **Getting a prize, some praise or a reward**
- **Making yourself happy or proud**

Now take a look at that list.

What do lots of them have in common?

They're about wanting to do well for things or people **outside** of you. It's about making them happy and being concerned about what they will think. That's called 'external motivation'.

The last one is about what's **inside** you and that's called 'internal motivation'. It's the most important because if _you_ care, you will find the drive to make more effort when things are difficult, to keep going when it hurts, to wrestle with a problem even when it baffles you. It also means that when you have achieved something good, you're not guessing about what someone else is thinking or feeling – you already know. And that's the best motivation of all.

> *Of course, even with the best motivation in the world, sometimes things don't go right ...*

⇒ CARE LESS OR CARE MORE? ⇐

Trying to find your motivation again after a setback is tricky.

When I first went back to school after being suspended for shoplifting, I felt cut off from everyone else and completely isolated. I couldn't bear the rejection. As a defence, I pretended I didn't care. But pretending not to care can fast become a habit. Before long I found myself hiding behind pillars in dark corners of the school where no one would see me. I stayed quiet in class, afraid of getting something wrong and looking like an idiot. I struggled to get up in the morning, asking myself,

'What's the point?'

I didn't feel like smiling and I certainly didn't laugh.

My schoolwork started to suffer but I kept saying to myself,

'I DON'T CARE.'

I WAS TRYING TO GET THROUGH IT ALL ON MY **OWN.**

me

But hiding my true feelings was tough because, deep down, I did care. I *wanted* to make friends again, I *wanted* to be liked, I *wanted* not to be bottom of every set and I *wanted* to be selected for the teams in PE.

I wanted to be a BETTER version of me.

I wish I could tell you that there was a quick fix to the problem I faced. I don't remember reading a book with all the answers or listening to a song that inspired me to pick myself up, although I probably did both. I do remember being helped. A girl in my year started being nice to me. Antonia offered to sit next to me in class when no one else would. Having a friend made all the difference.

I started to smile and laugh again.

Antonia is still my friend today. In fact, she's having one of the kittens that are in the box beside my desk. She has called him Freddie.

⋛ FOCUS ON FOCUSING ⋚

Something else that really helped me during this time was sport. I could be someone else when I was playing a game. I was a position, not a person. The rest of the team had to include me because those were the rules. The game also gave me a way of escape. I concentrated so hard on the game itself that nothing else mattered.

You may *love*

cycling *singing* ROCK CLIMBING

HIKING PLAYING
VIDEO GAMES

reading

PAINTING

and feel that same emotion.

You're lost in what is happening right now and it's all that matters.

In the hobbies that we pick, the books that we read or the films we watch, the ones that we enjoy most are the ones that hold our attention.

They keep us gripped.

Think about the times when you have been so happy that it seemed as if time sped up. The day went too fast and suddenly everything is a blur. You can't remember every minute of what you did or how you did it, but you know you enjoyed it.

This feeling of losing yourself in something is one of the best motivations going. It means that you'll return to your hobby again and again. If you're looking for something to become really good at, just think about what activity made a day speed by in a flash.

YOU'LL HAVE ALL THE MOTIVATION YOU NEED – WITHOUT EVEN TRYING!

GAME CHANGERS

Who knew that diving into the ocean could lead to a lifelong passion for saving planet Earth? But this is exactly what happened to Dutch inventor *Boyan Slat*. When he was a boy in Greece, he was diving deep beneath the waves and was horrified to see so much plastic pollution among the wildlife down there. He became determined to do something about it. He'd found his motivation to help the planet –

just by wearing his swimming trunks!

Slat set up The Ocean Cleanup, a non-profit organisation devoted to cleaning up all the oceans in the world. Their aim is to remove 90 per cent of the nasty, mucky, fatal-to-fish plastics that have been thoughtlessly chucked into the ocean. He has even invented a clean-up system called The Interceptor, which sounds like a superhero and it sort of is. It prevents the flow of plastic pollution into the ocean. Boyan Slat and his swimming trunks are changing the world.

'WHATEVER YOUR GOAL ... , YOU CAN GET THERE – AS LONG AS YOU'RE **WILLING** TO BE **HONEST** WITH YOURSELF ABOUT THE **PREPARATION** AND **WORK** INVOLVED'.

OPRAH WINFREY, ACTOR, TV PRESENTER, PRODUCER, AUTHOR

⇒ THEY SAID I COULDN'T, ⇐
BUT I SAID I COULD!

Have you ever had someone tell you that you can't do something?

I have.

My careers teacher at school told me that I wouldn't be able to go to university. The worst of it? She was right. My grades weren't good enough. So I gave up and went to sit in my bedroom, sulking.

**ARE YOU KIDDING?
OF COURSE, I DIDN'T!**

I was determined to prove my teacher wrong!

I studied harder than ever before and re-took my exams. I wanted to do better. And guess what? _I did._ I improved my grades and got into university. The experience taught me that when people say you can't do something, it's up to you to prove them right or prove them wrong. If you are driven enough to try something and fail –

TRY AGAIN.

Then you are giving yourself a second chance of success.

My teacher's negative comments gave me the motivation that I needed to **work hard**. Ever since then, I know that if someone says something rubbish about me, I can use it to my advantage.

IT WORKS AS MOTIVATION.

But it also cancels out the negative. It makes me feel in control of the situation and that I'm deciding how I react. It doesn't mean I don't get offended or upset (that still happens even now), but I try to channel my emotion into something positive.

Why don't you try it?

BE A TIME TRAVELLER

I'm going to trust you now with another secret ...

The secret to **MY** motivation.

It's easy to be motivated when you're doing something you _love_. But what about when it's homework in your least favourite subject, or if you're asked to wash the dishes or tidy your room?

How do you motivate yourself then?

An idea I use is to look into the future! Be a time traveller and leap ahead to imagine what the results of finishing your task will be. You could even write down your motivation in a journal or notebook. Then think of a treat for when you achieve that goal. It may be a bike ride or practising some football tricks, but you absolutely cannot have it until you have completed the task.

But you still need to get through the task.

So how do you do that?

Well, you can pair the activity you don't want to do with one that you like. Here are some twinned activities you could choose from:

* **Have your favourite music playing in the background while you tidy your pit of a bedroom (believe me, this one works)**

* **Go for a walk while practising your class presentation (this is something I do a lot, by the way!)**

* **Stroke your pet while memorising stuff for your science test tomorrow**

* **Listen to an audiobook on your headphones while doing the dishes**

* **Use your favourite pens for homework (I've got a really LOVELY set of highlighter pens that I use for my TV presentation prep!)**

SLOWLY BUT SURELY, YOUR TASK WILL GET DONE. AND WHEN YOU HAVE ACHIEVED THIS GOAL, ENJOY IT AND THEN REMEMBER THE FEELING OF MOTIVATION FOR NEXT TIME.

CAKE OF KINDNESS

9

'Be kind whenever possible.
It is always possible.'

THE DALAI LAMA

I honestly believe that animals reflect back to us the best of our nature.

They can also reflect back the worst of us.

Many of the animals I grew up with were bigger and stronger than me.
If they don't want to do something, they won't do it. You can try to

guide them with a lead, but you have to learn to persuade them to do something *with* you, not for you.

No dog or cat (or guinea pig or pony for that matter) is born with **badness** inside it. They mirror our treatment of them. So if we are patient, consistent and kind, they will do things for us because they want to. If we are angry, violent and unpredictably cruel, they will do things out of fear and ultimately bite or kick in protest.

As you know by now, I grew up with horses. The kindest horse I ever knew was a big, chunky chestnut called Stuart. He was born at our home and he loved people, particularly women, from day one. He seemed to always know if I was feeling sad and needed a hug. I remember pushing my face into his neck, hugging his huge shoulders, and he put his head over my back and held me until I stopped crying.

He was huge but so soft and gentle, both with me and with smaller horses. When he was older he would look after foals who had been weaned from their mothers. He lay with them at night and looked after them during the day, teaching them how to respect each other and play without being too rough.

My childhood experiences with animals taught me some of the more important lessons about kindness that I've carried with me through the rest of my life:

✴ Kindness doesn't have a pecking order or a ranking system.
✴ Be kind to everyone you meet.
✴ Give out kindness and you'll get it back. Trust me, this works.
✴ Kindness has a ripple effect. If you are kind to someone, in turn they'll be kind to someone else. It's like handing on a relay baton in a race.
✴ Kindness helps us to **_like ourselves_** as well as other people.
✴ Kindness affects the happiness of others (animal or human!). This is powerful stuff.

WHY WOULDN'T YOU USE KINDNESS FOR GOOD?

⋛ BAKING THE CAKE OF KINDNESS ⋚

Now, I love my fruit and veg, but I have to admit that one of my very favourite things to eat as a treat is cake.

> And I have a theory that being kind is like baking a cake.

Think about it. Baking is a science! Get the essential ingredients or measurements wrong and your cake will come out as flat as a, erm, pancake (which is not a cake, it just has 'cake' in its name). Get the ingredients right and something **magical** happens in the oven. Under the heat grows a glorious, fluffy and delicious cake that you can enjoy and share with other people. We use cakes to celebrate birthdays, weddings and lots of special occasions. A cake is *edible kindness* – but you have to get the measure of ingredients right …

There may be messages posted up around your school or online urging you to

but how much have any of us thought about what that really means? Yes, it means not starting a fight, not being mean to someone, not excluding someone; but what can you **actually** do to show that you ARE kind, and is it something you can get better at?

158

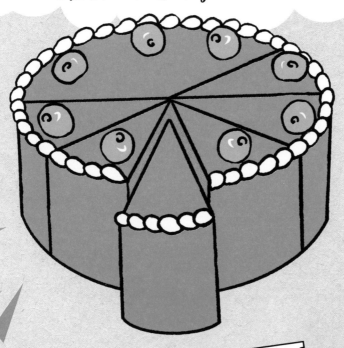

If we were making a Cake of Kindness, what would the ingredients be?

PATIENCE:

Like butter, patience is one of the **_essential_** ingredients for your Cake of Kindness. You'll see from Chapter 2 this can be hard to learn, but it is so worth it. My top tip is to wait as long as it takes for someone to accept your offer of help. Like baking itself, patience takes practice!

PATIENCE

LISTENING:

Allowing someone else to talk and making the time to truly listen. Active listening is a skill that involves shutting off your own thoughts, and devoting your mind and energy to what someone else is saying **without** interrupting! (I confess I find this bit *really* difficult ...)

FLOUR POWER

PHYSICAL SUPPORT:

Carrying, holding a hand, hugging, helping out – all of these show kindness and consideration. This is like the baking powder in your cake. It helps your cake (or in this case, **you**) to rise up and support your friends!

PHYSICAL SUPPORT

LENDING YOUR VOICE:

Speaking up for someone else to show them that you care and you are behind them. Putting your feelings into words isn't always easy, but your friends can't read your mind, no matter how brilliant they are!

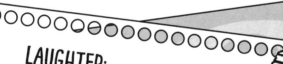

SHARING:

Even if you don't have enough, sharing is a sign of kindness and respect.

LAUGHTER:

I'm a **huge** believer in the power of laughter as a way to spread kindness around. It feels great to be able to make someone burst into giggles or produce a big, beaming smile. For me, this is the cherry on the cake!

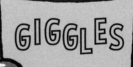

BE KIND TO YOURSELF

Sharing is _amazing_, but remember to save some cake for you!

DON'T FORGET, TO BE KIND TO YOURSELF.

Whenever anything bad or embarrassing happens to me, I find that taking some time for myself, stepping away from screens and nourishing my mind is the best thing ever. I find that writing things down in a diary or journal really helps to process my thoughts. I don't let anyone else read it (apart from my nosy cat, Button) but I find it can help me get some distance from all the things going in my head, and can feel like a bit of a 'spring clean' of the mind!

Button

⋛ FRIENDS, FRIENDS, FRIENDS ⋚

My best friend when I was young was called Heather. Both of her parents worked with mine looking after the horses.

Heather and I went to primary school together until I was 10. She was kind and funny, she liked horses and dogs, and we lived right next door to each other. We pretended to ride our ponies around imaginary cross-country courses that we built out of boxes and branches. I had tea at her house and we spent all our time together.

> Everyone needs a friend like that, right?

Then I went off to boarding school. It was never the same after that. I was so busy trying to keep up with my new classmates that I abandoned Heather. I have always felt bad about that. Unfortunately, I turned into a snob overnight and I ignored the qualities that had made her my friend.

So, learn from my mistakes.

DON'T DO THAT.

Sometimes you turn into the person you think you're meant to be around certain people, instead of just being

you.

I started to show off in front of my new friends. I turned into a bit of a brat and it makes me shudder to think about it.

Looking back, I didn't understand that not everybody has the same **opportunities** or the same **advantages,** and that actually I was really lucky.

I FELT ASHAMED.

And eventually, I worked out that the best friends to have were people I liked and admired – not the people at my new school that I was trying to impress. People like Heather. Fortunately for me, she forgave me, and we became friends again.

But that's why it's so important to have friends with different backgrounds, who go to different schools or who like different things.

HAVE A THINK.

What do you love about your best friend?

'He looks after me when I'm down.'

'She's SO kind and shares her stuff with me.'

'He's so funny and invites me over!'

'He supports me, especially if there's something I don't understand in class.'

'She makes me roll about laughing.'

'She sticks up for me if other people are being nasty.'

When you think about the things you admire in your best friend, often they will be the same things they admire in you. Those qualities are never to do with what you look like, what you're wearing, what music you like or how your hair is styled. Those things are just decoration, they're not part of the actual cake.

> **What they really love is your character and your personality.**

Don't be frightened of being challenged or disagreeing with your friends. Debate is healthy and it means you're thinking about things, not just taking them for granted. And take it from me, however isolated you might feel, there will always be a friend or group of friends for you.

And if you are the one looking out for others who might need a friend, **you** are even more likely to find them.

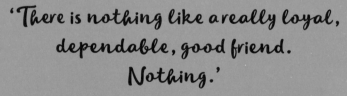

'There is nothing like a really loyal, dependable, good friend. Nothing.'
JENNIFER ANISTON, *FRIENDS* ACTOR.

GAME CHANGERS

As a 14-year-old, Australian **James Harrison** needed a blood donation when he had a lung operation. He benefitted from the blood someone else had given and so he learned first-hand how important is to help others – even people you don't know!

Then it was discovered he had a set of unique antibodies that could save lives. His blood contains Anti-D, which helps babies fight off blood cells that attack their developing bodies. So he decided to do something with his rare antibodies and donated his blood regularly over the course of more than 60 years. In that time, he made over a thousand donations and helped 2.4 million Australian babies stay healthy.

His experience as a teenager taught him to be selfless, empathetic and kind – he became a life-saver.

WHO KNOWS?

MAYBE YOU HAVE A SECRET INSIDE OF YOU THAT CAN HELP OTHERS!

Sometimes we are led to believe that to be successful in life, we have to be ruthless and ambitious. We hear phrases used like 'the survival of the fittest' or that you've got to 'look after number one', suggesting that being kind is somehow a sign of weakness.

BUT I THINK IT IS BRAVER, STRONGER AND MORE POWERFUL TO BE KIND.

If the world is to flourish, I think KINDNESS should be at the heart of everything we do.

And it's more important now than it ever has been.

10 WAYS TO BE KINDER ... AND HAPPIER

1. *Always* say thank you

2. **Ask if you can give someone a hug** you never know when you might need one back

3. **Share what you have** sharing is caring, right?

4. **Offer to help** don't wait to be asked!

5. **Say sorry** the hardest word, but the most important

6. **Offer a compliment** it costs nothing, and everyone loves them!

7. **Smile at someone** if nothing else, you'll enjoy the oxytocin (a chemical released in the brain that makes you feel awesome about yourself ...)

8. **Be gentle with animals** they ask for nothing else (well, apart from lots of food, if my cat is anything to go by ...)

9. **Don't react to something in anger** anger and frustration are a waste of your precious energy; focus it elsewhere

10. **Give your friend your time** *time is free!*

FINALLY, WRITE DOWN THREE KIND THINGS YOU HAVE SAID OR DONE TODAY. IT WILL ENCOURAGE YOU TO DO MORE TOMORROW.

HOW TO GET BACK ON ....

10

*If I fall over and make mistakes,
I'll pick myself up and hope for the
best and try to conduct myself with as
much authenticity and moral code'.*

**NICOLE KIDMAN,
ACTOR AND PRODUCER**

As you will know by now, I'm no stranger
to failure. I've had a few fails and falls
in my life – as will you, and every one of
the 7.8 billion of us on the planet.

LET'S FACE IT,
IT'S PART
OF BEING
HUMAN.

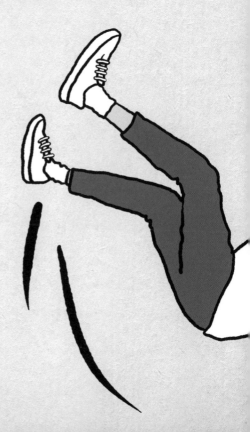

But it doesn't matter how many times you've failed. It matters WAAAAY more about how you get back up and keep going.

So how do you talk to yourself about 'falling off'?

Do you let your shoulders drop, wallow in your misery, let your fall (or your 'fail') dominate your thoughts, talk about it all the time and generally let it make you miserable?

OR

DO YOU SHAKE YOURSELF DOWN, GIVE YOURSELF A GOOD TALKING-TO, PULL YOUR SHOULDERS BACK AND CLIMB RIGHT **BACK ON** TO GIVE WHATEVER IT WAS ANOTHER **TRY?**

⋛ NEGATIVE NO-NO ⋚

Do you know our brains are capable of up to *60,000* thoughts a day? That's a lot of different things whizzing through our heads.

But.

DID YOU ALSO KNOW THAT 80 PER CENT OF THOSE THOUGHTS WILL BE NEGATIVE?

I am as guilty as anyone of latching on to the one bad thing someone has said and not letting go. Whether it's a casual remark from a colleague, something that I've seen online that bugs me, or a thoughtless sideswipe from my brother, it can really get under my skin.

So how do I pick myself up?

Well, I've got to tell you that music is a real mood-changer. Pick your favourite happy song, stick on your headphones and **sing!** I listen to music all the time – when I'm travelling, when I'm writing, when I'm walking – and it never fails to lift me up. The upbeat songs give me energy, make me want to dance, make me want to grab someone I love and give them a hug.

173

⋛ WORD OF THE WEEK ⋚

Have you ever thought about how **_powerful_** language can be? Words can make all the difference, whether you're saying them to yourself or to someone else. Have you ever thought about the power of a word?

Take a moment and think about these:

Adventure POSITIVITY

Freedom

BUMFUZZLE
(this brilliant word means 'to get confused'!)

Think about each of these words in turn. I bet each of these words conjure an image in your mind, right?

So, what if you took the power of words and turned them into a **_fantastic tool_** to help you get back on after making a mistake?

All you need is a notebook (yay! stationery!) – maybe add some colourful stickers if you want to jazz it up.

Each week, sit down and open up the notebook so that you have a left-hand and a right-hand page open. Think about the **word** you'd like to focus on for the next seven days. It could be a noun, a verb or an adjective.

For example:

Grace
Courage
Energetic
Gentle
Champion
Relaxed
Spontaneous
Thoughtful

Write your word down on the left-hand page in nice big letters. Throughout the week, each day write down on the facing page what this word has motivated you to achieve. By the end of the year, you'll have a notebook full of achievements.

ALL FROM 52 SIMPLE WORDS.

Maybe you can even make a poster of your

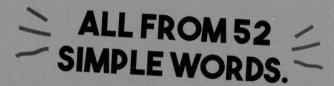

YEAR OF WORDS!

GAME CHANGERS

In 2008, *J.K. Rowling* gave a speech at Harvard University. Everyone was probably expecting the author of the Harry Potter books to speak about creativity and success. Instead, she spoke about *failure*. She described herself seven years after her own graduation as having been the biggest failure she knew.

It was her greatest fear to be poor, jobless, divorced and bringing up her daughter on her own, and yet she says that reaching that point, where all those things were her reality, was the beginning of starting to get back on and keep going.

'ROCK BOTTOM BECAME THE SOLID FOUNDATION ON WHICH I REBUILT MY LIFE.'

The Harry Potter books are the best-selling book series of all time, with over 500 million copies sold in 80 languages worldwide. J.K. Rowling is the most famous living author. She isn't just successful, she is a record-breaker, the best of the best, the top of the pile.

J.K. Rowling believes in the importance of knowing and embracing failure. On falling off and getting back on.

'Failure is so important. We speak about success all the time. But it is the ability to resist or use failure that often leads to greater success.'

J.K. ROWLING, AUTHOR

'I HAVEN'T FAILED, I'VE JUST FOUND 10,000 WAYS THAT DON'T WORK.'

THOMAS EDISON,
THE INVENTOR OF THE LIGHT BULB FAILED MANY TIMES
BEFORE HE PERFECTED HIS INVENTION.

⋛ STAYING POWER! ⋚

Sportspeople have to live with losing matches, races or games every day of their lives. It's part of their job to **learn from it**. They have to analyse their mistakes, take on board criticism and move forward to a better performance next time. Their coach will be honest (in some cases brutally honest!) in their feedback on what they did right and wrong.

 **Michael Jordan**, the legendary US basketball player, knows exactly how many matches he has lost and how many times he missed the winning shot. He reckons he's missed over 9,000 shots in total and it is a result of all those misses and all those matches lost that has made him a success.

HE DOESN'T LET THE 'FALLS' GET HIM DOWN, INSTEAD HE USES THEM TO HELP HIM 'GET BACK ON'.

You will often hear an athlete talk about 'taking the positives' from a defeat or a disappointing show. This is because positive thoughts give you energy and negative ones take it away. It's important to realise that failure can be a feeling rather than an actual outcome. You feel low, you think you're no good at something, so you can't see the point of having a go. Then you feel worse.

IT'S REALLY IMPORTANT TO CATCH YOURSELF BEFORE YOU FALL INTO THAT NEGATIVE SPIRAL OF THOUGHTS!

Know that you *can* recover, because the opposite of that negative spiral is also true. If you feel happy and positive, you will have more energy to achieve and do the things you want to do.

HAPPY POSITIVE ENERGY

GAME CHANGERS

Tony Hudgell had suffered terrible injuries when he was a baby and had to have both his legs amputated. He was only five years old when he decided to take on a fundraising challenge inspired by **Captain Tom Moore**, who in 2020 walked 100 laps of his garden using a walking frame in the build-up to his 100th birthday. Tony, 95 years younger than him, said:

'I CAN do that.'

So he walked every day in the month of June until he reached 10 kilometres.

Tony wanted to raise money for the hospital where the doctors and nurses had saved his life. He had only just had his prosthetic legs delivered when he started the challenge, so he was still learning how to use them, but every day he got **stronger** and **better** at walking.

Tony ended up raising over £1.2 million for the hospital. The inspiring stories of both Captain Tom and Tony Hudgell show that just putting one foot in front of the other is the extraordinary power behind keeping going.

HOW TO WIN AT BEING WRONG

OK, let's be honest, it's human nature to want to be right, isn't it?

As a result, we are often very sensitive to goofing up, messing up, getting things wrong and making blunders. So this is a game I like to play sometimes to remind me that being wrong, falling off or making mistakes is

ACTUALLY.
JUST.
FINE.

The aim of the game is to make as many mistakes as possible. You're not allowed to get an answer right. So if I say, 'What's the capital of France?' you say any city you can think of **EXCEPT** 'Paris'.

OK. Let's give it a go.

1. what's the biggest city in the UK?

2. what do you put on toast?

3. what's a baby dog called?

4. How many legs does an octopus have?

5. Name a citrus fruit?

It's funny how quickly your brain will go for the right answer and then you have to readjust to think of a wrong one. It makes me laugh to come up with ridiculous answers like 'mud' for question 2 or 'chocolate' for question 5, and that's the point – if we can laugh at getting things wrong, at falling off or failing, the mistakes don't seem so serious.

HOW TO KEEP
GOING

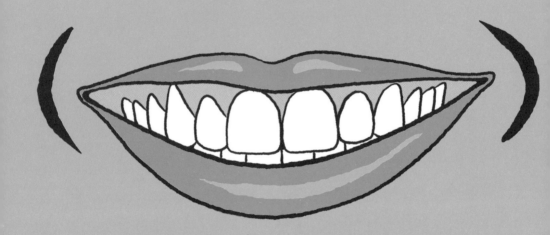

AND KEEP
GROWING

By now I hope you'll be busy doing some of the exercises, and following some of the tips and activities to help you build your courage, your **creativity** or your **stickability**! Don't feel you have to do them all at once.

Take it steady,
tackle one thing at a time.

Some of my thoughts, tips and suggestions will work for you, others won't – and that's fine.

DO THE ONES
THAT MAKE
YOU FEEL GOOD!

1

If you need a quick reminder of some of the things we've talked about, here are my top 10 takeaways for being at the top of your game:

Don't beat yourself up over **mistakes, fails or falls.** Trust me, I have lain awake in bed for nights on end going over and over a gaffe or mistake I've made on TV. It doesn't help you at all (in fact, all it does is make me really tired and grumpy). Though your goof-up might seem like

THE ONLY THING

everyone is thinking about, believe me when I say that **NO ONE ELSE** will even remember it. And do remember this also, if you want to be **good** at something, **you will fall off**. It's an inevitable part of trying hard and doing your best! Just be honest with yourself about it and be open with others if you can. If you don't want to talk about it, at least tell your dog, cat or gerbil. They won't judge you, they will still love you – and you'll feel better for getting it out there and saying it out loud.

PATIENCE IS YOUR SUPERPOWER!

Patience is not expecting everything to happen at once, but exercising self-control and doing things with focus and care. I struggled with patience and insecurity when I was young, but I've learned so much about it from inspirational people around me and people that I admire from afar. I hope some of the people you've read about in this book inspire you!

3

Pull on your

CLOAK OF
CONFIDENCE

first thing in the morning and let it power you confidently throughout your day. I pull on my own invisible 'cloak' and often do a confident 'power pose' before talking to a large audience, presenting on TV, or doing anything that challenges me.

It really works!

4

Ditch those old **Pretending Pants** and flex your **muscles of courage** so that you can try new and exciting things, stick up for other people, but also have the courage to

BE YOURSELF.

USE YOUR CREATIVITY TO CHANGE THE 10 METRES AROUND YOURSELF. TRY TO COME UP WITH THREE FANTASTICALLY GREAT IDEAS TO MAKE THE WORLD A SAFER, CLEANER, KINDER, HAPPIER PLACE!

STAND UP
AND
SPEAK OUT

for what you **believe in** and for what **matters** to you most. And don't forget to use positive and open body language, and maintain eye contact with the people you are speaking to. Get into this habit, and trust me, you'll feel more powerful!

7

Being

STRETCHY

and

benɑy

will really help you adapt to big and small changes and help you get the most out of life.

And remember

ANYTHING IS POSSIBLE!

The only thing stopping us
(most of the time, anyway) is

OURSELVES.

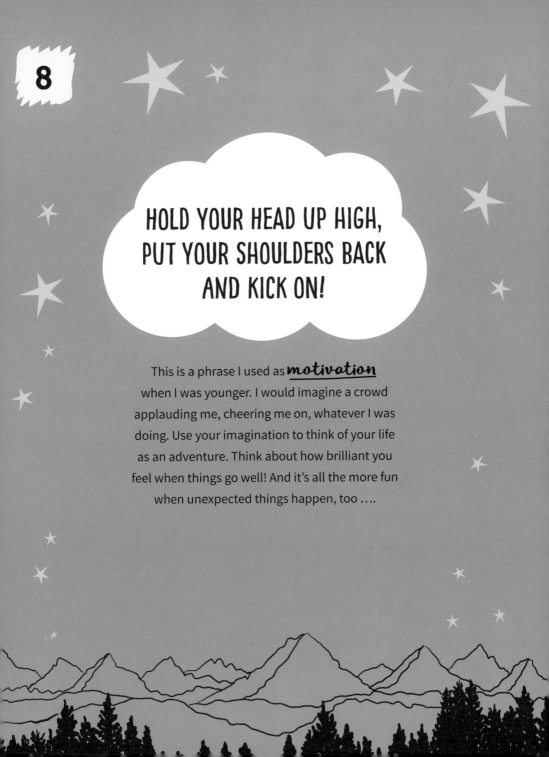

8

HOLD YOUR HEAD UP HIGH, PUT YOUR SHOULDERS BACK AND KICK ON!

This is a phrase I used as **motivation** when I was younger. I would imagine a crowd applauding me, cheering me on, whatever I was doing. Use your imagination to think of your life as an adventure. Think about how brilliant you feel when things go well! And it's all the more fun when unexpected things happen, too ….

Bake a *Cake of Kindness* to share
with someone who needs a helping hand
or support in some way.

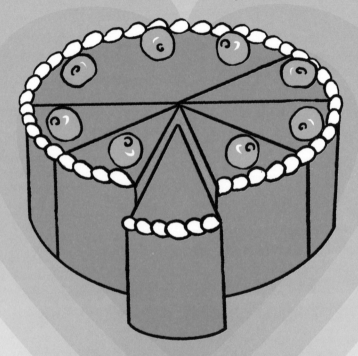

KINDNESS
is everything.

10

When things seem tough, just put one foot in front of the other, ***one step at a time***. Don't focus on anything too far away or too big, just concentrate on moving forward, because the best advice when you fall off is …

Index

References

Serena Williams
Williams, Serena. 'The fall and rise of maturing Serena Williams'. *The National*, 10 September 2012 (spoken statement). https://www.thenational.ae/sport/the-fall-and-rise-of-maturing-serena-williams-1.632294, accessed 30 September 2020.

Sky Brown
Brown, Sky. https://www.instagram.com/tv/CA5_AfhgdhH/?utm_source=ig_embed, accessed 30 September 2020.

Bill Gates
Gates, Bill. Patience is a key element of Success. Independently published, 2020.

Roger Federer
Federer, Roger. Interview with Colin McDonald for True.Ink. https://true.ink/story/roger-federer-peaceful-tennis-place/, accessed 30 September 2020.

David Attenborough
Attenborough, David. 'David Attenborough on the moments that made his heart leap'. RTÉ Radio 1, 12 October 2018 (spoken statement). https://www.rte.ie/lifestyle/living/2018/1012/1002676-david-attenborough-on-the-moments-that-made-his-heart-leap/, accessed 30 September 2020.

Sam Kerr
Kerr, Sam. 'There are no hierarchies, no cliques … we are fit and we are fast'. The Guardian.com, 23 August 2017 (reported statement). https://www.theguardian.com/football/2017/aug/24/sam-kerr-when-the-goals-come-you-have-more-fun-its-a-ripple-effect, accessed 30 September 2020.

Venus Williams
Williams, Venus. 'Venus Williams Courts Success in Fashion, Fun … and Tennis' ABC NEWS, 25 April 2013 https://abcnews.go.com/blogs/headlines/2013/04/venus-williams-courts-success-in-fashion-fun-and-tennis, accessed 30 September 2020.

Usain Bolt

Bolt, Usain. 'Bolt and Blake ease into 200m final'. ABC News, 8 August 2012 (reported statement). https://www.abc.net.au/news/2012-08-09/bolt2c-blake-to-battle-for-200-gold/4186836, accessed 30 September 2020.

Megan Rapinoe

Rapinoe, Megan. Twitter.com, 5 January 2020. https://twitter.com/TheWomensOrg/status/1213747090662313985, accessed 30 September 2020.

Edmund Hillary

Johnstone, Alexa. *Sir Edmund Hillary: An Extraordinary Life*. London: Penguin, 2008.

Bethany Hamilton

Hamilton, Bethany. *Soul Surfer: A True Story of Faith, Family, and Fighting to Get Back on the Board*. MTV Books, 2007.

Maya Angelou

Angelou, Maya. Interview with *The Bell Telephone Magazine*, Volume 61, Number 1, 1982.

James Dyson

Dyson, James. The James Dyson Foundation (reported statement). https://www.facebook.com/JamesDysonFoundation/posts/good-ideas-can-come-at-any-time-so-always-have-a-pencil-to-hand-james-dyson-for-/10155672709498608/, accessed 30 September 2020.

Malala Yousafzai

Yousafzai, Malala. *I Am Malala: How One Girl Stood Up for Education and Changed the World*. London: Orion Children's Books 2015

Coco Gauff

Gauff, Coco. 'My generation has just decided it is time to speak up'. *The Guardian*, 16 October 2019 (reported statement). https://www.theguardian.com/sport/2019/oct/16/coco-gauff-wimbledon-generation-tennis, accessed 30 September 2020.

Michelle Obama

Obama, Michelle. Remarks by The First Lady...in a Discussion with Howard University Students, The White House, 1 September 2016 (reported statement). https://obamawhitehouse.archives.gov/the-press-office/2016/09/01/remarks-first-lady-nick-cannon-and-seth-meyers-discussion-howard, accessed 30 September 2020.

Tina Fey

Fey, Tina. *Bossypants*. London: Little, Brown Book Group, 2011.

Oprah Winfrey

Winfrey, Oprah. 'What I know for sure'. Oprah.com (reported statement). https://www.oprah.com/omagazine/what-i-know-for-sure-hard-work, accessed 30 September 2020.

Jennifer Aniston

Aniston, Jennifer. 'There's nothing like a loyal friend. Nothing'. *Now to Love*, 29 October 2019 (reported statement). https://www.nowtolove.co.nz/lifestyle/career/jennifer-aniston-importance-of-good-loyal-friends-43698, accessed 30 September 2020.

Nicole Kidman

Kidman, Nicole. Nicole Kidman Official Facebook page, 9 May 2016 (reported statement). https://www.facebook.com/NicoleKidmanOfficial/photos/pb.344294141127.-2207520000.1463414116./10153482428136128, accessed 30 September 2020.

J. K. Rowling

Rowling, J.K. Commencement Speech at Harvard University, 2008 (spoken statement).

J. K. Rowling

Rowling, J.K. The Oprah Winfrey Show, 2010 (spoken statement).

Thomas Edison

Dyer, Frank Lewis and Martin, Thomas Commerford. *Edison: His Life and Inventions*. New York: Harper & Brothers, 1910.

Acknowledgements

There are lots of people to thank for making this book possible but first of all, if it's OK with you, I'd like to thank the animals.

Thanks to Valkyrie for teaching me how to fall off without hurting my pride and most importantly, how to get back on again. Thanks to Flossy for teaching me patience and Frank the pony for showing me that it's OK to be really different. Thanks to Archie the Tibetan Terrier who was a huge part of our lives for over 15 years and to Button and the kittens for giving us cuddles when we needed them and showing us how to laugh again. Thanks to all the birds in the sky, the fish in the sea and all the animals on land for showing us that it's only us humans who over-complicate our emotions with daft things like insecurity, ego or envy.

As for the good human beings who have helped turn thoughts into reality, the first thank you is to Jessica Holm whose illustrations have brought this book to life. We have known each other a long time and it has long been a dream of mine for us to team up, so I'm really glad it has finally worked out. That's all because my editor Debbie Foy and Creative Director Sophie Stericker saw the brilliance of Jess's artwork and agreed that she was the right illustrator to make the words leap off the page. Debbie has also helped me shape my ideas into something that makes more sense, has encouraged me every step of the way and given me a kick up the backside when needed.

Laura and Claire have designed a book that is beautiful and full of energy and I thank them for that, as well as Kelly for the production. Rebecca and Fi have spread the word with their devotion to PR and marketing and thank you also to Garance for negotiating the rights.

For those of you who decide to write books of your own, having a supercharged, intelligent and savvy literary agent is essential. Eugenie Furniss is the best – she always believed this was a good idea and took me to Hachette to make it happen. She and Emily MacDonald at 42 have been so supportive every step of the way, so a big high five to them.

All in all it's been a terrific team effort and very much in the spirit of this book, we have looked out for each other and always offered a helping hand.

Most of all, big thanks to YOU for reading it. I really hope this book makes you feel supported and strengthened. It can be a tough old world sometimes but there is so much to enjoy, cherish and embrace and I want you to revel in it all. I used to have a diary with a quote on the front page that really helped me:

"Life isn't about waiting for the storm to pass, it's about learning to dance in the rain."

So come on, let's BOOGIE together!